# NON-MEANS　BENEFITS: THE LEGISLATION

# SUPPLEMENT 1997

### Commentary by

**DAVID BONNER,** LL.B., LL.M.
*Senior Lecturer in Law, University of Leicester
Member, Social Security Appeal Tribunals*

**IAN HOOKER,** LL.B.
*Lecturer in Law, University of Nottingham
Member, Social Security Appeal Tribunals*

**ROBIN WHITE,** M.A., LL.M.
*Professor of Law, University of Leicester
Deputy Social Security Commissioner*

Up to date to October 1, 1997

London
Sweet & Maxwell
1997

Published in 1997 by
Sweet & Maxwell Limited, of
100 Avenue Road,
London NW3 3PF
http://www.smlawpub.co.uk
Typeset by
Wyvern 21 Ltd,
Bristol
Printed in England by
Clays Ltd,
St Ives plc

No natural forests were destroyed to make this product; only farmed timber was used and replanted.

**Main Work ISBN 0-421-607505**
**Supplement ISBN 0-421-607602**

A CIP catalogue record for this book is available from the British Library.

All rights reserved. U.K. statutory material in this publication is acknowledged as Crown copyright.

No part of this publication may be reproduced or transmitted in any form or by any means, or stored in a retrieval system of any nature without prior written permission, except for permitted fair dealing under the Copyright, Designs and Patents Act 1988, or in accordance with the terms of a licence issued by the Copyright Licensing Agency in respect of photocopying and/or reprographic reproduction. Application for permission for other use of copyright material including permission for other use of copyright material including permission to reproduce extracts in other published works shall be made to the publishers. Full acknowledgement of author, publisher and source must be given.

©
D. Bonner, I. Hooker, and R. White
1997

# PAGES OF MAIN VOLUME AFFECTED BY MATERIAL IN THIS SUPPLEMENT

| Main volume page affected | Relevant page in Supplement |
|---|---|
| 23 | 3 |
| 34 | 3 |
| 36 | 3 |
| 46 | 4 |
| 50 | 4 |
| 61 | 4 |
| 106 | 5 |
| 135 | 5 |
| 151 | 5 |
| 165 | 5 |
| 168 | 6 |
| 196–199 | 6 |
| 212 | 9 |
| 221 | 9 |
| 267–268 | 9 |
| 358 | 10 |
| 376 | 11 |
| 426 | 13 |
| 436 | 13 |
| 440 | 13 |
| 622–638 | 13 |
| 644 | 28 |
| 647 | 28 |
| 649 | 29 |
| 654 | 29 |
| 655 | 30 |
| 668 | 31 |
| 920–922 | 31 |
| 934–935 | 31 |
| 936–938 | 32 |
| 937–938 | 32 |
| 943–944 | 32 |
| 951–952 | 32 |
| 952 | 37 |
| 953 | 40 |
| 953–954 | 41 |
| 1030 | 45 |
| 1039 | 45 |
| 1089 | 45 |
| 1089–1090 | 46 |
| 1109 | 47 |

# TABLE OF CASES

Insurance Officer v. McCaffrey [1984] 1 W.L.R. 1353; [1985] 1 All E.R. 5; (1984) S.J. 836; (1985) 82 L.S.Gaz, HL; affirming 3 N.I.J.B., CA ............................ 6
Nancollas v. Insurance Officer [1985] 1 All E.R. 833, CA ........................................ 7
Smith v. Stages [1989] A.C. 928; [1989] 2 W.L.R. 529; [1989] 1 All E.R. 833; (1989) 133 S.J. 324; [1989] I.C.R. 272; [1989] I.R.L.R. 177; (1989) 139 N.L.J. 291, HL ........................................................................................................ 7

# TABLE OF SOCIAL SECURITY COMMISSIONER'S DECISIONS

| | | | |
|---|---|---|---|
| CA/7126/1995 | 28 | CIB/14442/96 | 31, 32, 40 |
| CA/11185/1995 | 28 | CIB/14587/96 | 34 |
| CDLA 1304/95 | 6 | CIB/15235/96 | 31, 32 |
| CDLA 11099/96 | 30 | CIB/16237/96 | 44 |
| CF/12/94 | 9 | CIS/332/1993 | 4 |
| CF/7146/95 | 45 | CIS/12015/1996 | 3 |
| CG/11/94 | 8 | CIS/12022/1996 | 4 |
| CG/5425/95 | 5, 6 | CP/11496/95 | 5 |
| CI/696/49 | 46 | CS/7387/1959 | 3 |
| CI/94/94 | 9, 47 | CS/879/1995 | 3 |
| CI/156/94 | 46 | CS/12054/1996 | 3 |
| CI/160/94 | 46 | CSG/6/95 | 5 |
| CI/227/94 | 46 | CSG/7/96 | 5 |
| CI/514/94 | 46 | CSIB/14/96 | 41 |
| CI/600/94 | 9, 47 | CSIB/17/96 | 33 |
| CI/514/95 | 46 | CSS/71/1994 | 3 |
| CI/5408/95 | 46 | R(F)2/95 | 9 |
| CI/12201/96 | 45 | R(F)2/96 | 45 |
| CI14111/96 | 6, 8 | R(G)1/95 | 5 |
| CI/6608/96 | 10 | R(G)2/95 | 8 |
| CI/537/97 | 10 | R(I)2/93 | 10, 47 |
| CI/1847/97 | 10 | R(I)3/93 | 10, 47 |
| CI/1896/97 | 10 | R(S)1/1983 | 3 |
| CIB/13161/96 | 35, 37, 44 | RI(I)677/52 | 7 |
| CIB/13508/96 | 35, 37, 44 | | |
| CIB/14202/96 | 32, 40 | *Northern Ireland* | |
| CIB/14332/96 | 33, 42, 43 | CI/95(1B) | 33—37 |
| CIB/14430/96 | 3, 32 | | |

# TABLE OF STATUTES

1992 Social Security Contributions and Benefits Act (c. 4)
s.2 .................................... 8
s.30C ........................... 37, 39
Sched. 7 ...........................
para. 13(1) ............... 10, 47
(8) ............... 10, 47
(10)(b) ............. 47

1997 Social Security Administration (Fraud) Act (c. 47) ................................. 5

# TABLE OF STATUTORY INSTRUMENTS

1996 Social Security (Industrial Injuries and Diseases) (miscellaneous Amendment) Regulations 1996 (S.I. 1996 No. 425) ...... 9
1997 Jobseeker's Allowance (Contract for Work) Regulations (S.I. 1997 No. 982) ................................ 10
Jobseeker's Allowance (Project Work Pilot Scheme) Regulations (S.I. 1997 No. 983) ...... 10
Social Security (United States of America) Order (S.I. 1997 No. 1778) ........................... 9

1997 Social Security (Attendance Allowance and Disability Living Allowance) (Miscellaneous Amendments) Regulations (S.I. 1997 No. 1839) ................. 13, 29, 31
Jobseeker's Allowance (Workskill Courses) Pilot (No. 2) Regulations (S.I. 1997 No. 1909) ............................. 10

v

## USING THIS SUPPLEMENT

1. For abbreviations please refer to the Table of Abbreviations at pp. xvii–xix of the main volume.

2. The amendments and updating contained in this Supplement are keyed into the page numbers of the main volume. Where there has been a significant number of changes to the legislation, the whole section, sub-section, paragraph or regulation, as amended, is set out in this Supplement. Other changes are noted by an instruction to insert or substitute new material or to delete part of the existing text. The date the change takes effect is also noted. Where explanation is needed of the change, or there is updating to be done to existing annotations but no change to the legislation, you will also find new annotations in this Supplement. The new annotations explain the new statutory material or take account of new cases or give prominence to certain points which seem to warrant more detailed attention.

You will need to use this Supplement alongside the main volume. You will find on p. iii a list of pages of the main volume which are affected by material in this Supplement. You may wish to use the list to mark pages of the main volume which need to be read in conjunction with updating material in this Supplement.

3. In the main volume at the end of each statute and set of regulations there is a list of statutes and statutory instruments taken into account in preparing the up-to-date text. You should add to those lists the additions noted at various points in this Supplement to give you an exact picture of the legislation taken into account in updating the main volume. That text, as amended by material noted in this Supplement, is now up to date to October 1, 1997.

## STOP PRESS

*The Social Security (Recovery of Benefits) Act 1997*

The Social Security (Recovery of Benefits) Act 1997 is brought into force on October 6, 1997 together with two sets of accompanying regulations: The Social Security (Recovery of Benefits) Regulations 1997 (S.I. 1997 No. 2205) and the Social Security (Recovery of Benefits) Appeals Regulations 1997 (S.I. 1997 No. 2237).

The Act re-states with amendments Part IV of the Contribution and Benefits Act, which is repealed. The Recovery of Benefit Regulations implement provisions of the Act, and the Recovery of Benefits Appeal Regulations deal with appeals to tribunals and leave to appeal to the Commissioner. The Appeal Regulations closely parallel provisions of the Adjudication Regulations.

# STATUTES

**p. 23,** *annotations to section 22*

A Tribunal of Commissioners has decided that it is the duty of tribunals when faced with a refusal of benefit on review of an open-ended claim for benefit to consider entitlement down to the date of the hearing. In each of three cases under appeal (*CIB/14430/1996, CIS/12015/1996* and *CS/12054/1996*) the tribunal had refused to take account of evidence that there had been a deterioration in the claimant's health after the date of the adjudication officer's decision. In so finding, the Commissioners disapprove decisions *CS/879/1995, CSS/71/1994* and *CS/7387/1959* ruling that a tribunal should not consider the position after the date of the adjudication officer's decision.

Taken together with *R(S)1/1983* the current position is that tribunals should take on board all issues down to the date of the appeal regardless of whether the decision under appeal is one arising on review by an adjudication officer or on an initial decision on benefit entitlement. As the Tribunal says in the common appendix to the three cases before them, such an approach reflects the way appellants view their appeals. They do not see the need for a fresh claim while their appeal is pending and it would seem wrong that they should be disadvantaged by simply waiting for the appeal decision (paragraph 12 of Common Appendix). The Commissioners recognise that in some cases, such an approach might require an adjournment to enable further evidence to be collected and put before the tribunal relating to the deterioration.

**p. 34,** *section 30*

With effect from July 1, 1997, new subsection (7A) is added to section 30 as follows:

> "(7A) The Secretary of State may undertake investigations to obtain information and evidence for the purposes of making applications under subsection (7) above."

**p. 36,** *section 32*

With effect from July 1, 1997, section 32(4)(b) is amended to read as follows:

"there has been supplied to the adjudication officer by the Secretary of State, or is otherwise available to him, information which gives him reasonable grounds for believing that entitlement to the component, or entitlement to it at the rate awarded or for that period ought not to continue."

**p. 46,** *section 57A*

With effect from July 1, 1997, new section 57A is inserted after section 57 as follows:

*"Medical examinations*

**Medical examinations of persons awarded attendance allowance or disability living allowance.**
**57A.**—Regulations may make provision—
  (a) enabling the Secretary of State to require a person to whom attendance allowance or disability living allowance has been awarded to submit to medical examination in prescribed circumstances;
  (b) for withholding payment of benefit in prescribed circumstances where a person has failed to submit himself to a medical examination to which he has been required to submit in accordance with regulations under paragraph (a) above; and
  (c) for the subsequent making in prescribed circumstances of payments withheld in accordance with regulations under paragraph (b) above."

**p. 50,** *section 61*

With effect from July 1, 1997, the words "under Part I of the Contributions and Benefits Act" are omitted.

**p. 61,** *annotations to section 71: appointees*

In *CIS/332/1993* Commissioner Mesher had suggested that where a person is acting as appointee, their acts are treated as the acts of the claimant, and if a question of recovering an overpayment arises from a failure by the appointee to disclose a material fact, then recovery should be from the claimant.

In *CIS/12022/1996* Commissioner Howell describes the distinction between a person in their capacity as appointee and in their personal capacity as "puzzling and metaphysical." In upholding the decision of a tribunal that an overpayment was recoverable from an appointee, the mother of the claimant who had failed to disclose increases in the claimant's savings the Commissioner appears to differ from Commissioner Mesher that the capacity in which a person acts affects the person from whom the overpayment is recoverable.

There is logic in both positions. Commissioner Mesher is making the point that an appointee's acts are those of the claimant who is unable to act for himself or herself. If a person is acting as appointee, then the recovery should be from the claimant. Commissioner Howell reflects the realities of daily life by noting that a person in the position of appointee will almost certainly not make clear distinctions between their capacity in dealing with the Department. If they should have disclosed something such as an increase in savings, then recovery can be sought from them, as well as from the claimant.

Since there is a difference of opinion between two Commissioners, tribunals are free to follow whichever of these two decisions they prefer.

**p. 106,** *amending statutes*

Add to the list of amending statutes Social Security Administration (Fraud) Act 1997, c.47.

**p. 135,** *annotations to section 38*

Decision *CSG/7/96* examines further the nature of marriage by habit and repute in Scotland. The parties had lived together for almost 20 years but never formally married. They had each been married previously and divorced, and that experience caused them both to be wary of remarriage. There was evidence that the couple were received in the community as a couple living in a stable relationship but none that they were taken to be married.

The Commissioner holds that the repute required to be shown is not confined to a general belief that the parties are formally married—it may suffice that people generally take them to be married in the sense that they accept all the usual consequences of marriage on an irregular basis. On the facts of this case, however, he found the evidence did not support the view that the parties were generally regarded as married even on that basis, and furthermore, that if they had been, their reluctance to introduce the formal ties of marriage would negative the necessary consent to living in a married state.

In *R(G) 1/95* the Commissioner found that a man, originally from Pakistan, who had come to live alone in the U.K. had acquired a domicile of choice in this country despite retaining a vague intention to return one day to Pakistan. In fact he did return there and married another wife before returning to U.K. with his second wife. When he died a claim for widow's allowance was made by his first wife, who had remained at all times in Pakistan. The Commissioner held she was entitled to succeed because having acquired a domicile of choice in the U.K. he could not contract a valid second marriage.

**p. 151,** *annotations to section 49*

Category B pensions are paid to a wife on the basis of her husband's contribution record. (And to a widower on the basis of his late wife's record under section 51). It follows that entitlement depends upon proof of a valid marriage and points concerning marriage arise here in the same way that they do in relation to Widow's Benefit—see section 38 and notes following.

In *CP/11496/95* the question concerned the validity of a marriage in the U.K. of a claimant whose husband had been previously married to another woman in India. The validity of their marriage depended upon the effectiveness of a *panchayat* divorce concluded in India in the absence of the husband. The Commissioner obtained an expert report (of which a copy is annexed to his decision) which confirmed the effectiveness of that divorce and thereby the validity of the second marriage.

**p. 165,** *annotations to section 70, subsections (5) and (6)*

A different approach on the question of late claims made by women past retirement age has been taken in decision *CSG/6/95*. The commissioner there rejects the robust approach adopted, *obiter*, in CG/5425/95, but reaches a similar conclusion, at least on the facts of the new case, by another route. The claimant had given up work in 1979 in order to care for her husband. She reached the retirement age for women (60) in December 1982, but under Directive 79/7 (which came into force in December 1984) would have remained entitled to claim until December 1987. In the meantime (September 1985) the U.K. law had been changed to require a claim to be made for entitlement to benefit to begin. The claimant eventually made her claim in November 1993 well past her 65th birthday. The Commissioner rejected the argument that had found favour in *CG/5425/95*, namely that the requirement to claim before that age could be ignored because of the continued non-compliance of U.K. domestic law. Instead, he held that the claimant had, in 1984, become "entitled" to benefit in accordance with *I. O. v. McCaffrey* [1985] 1 All E.R. 5 and that entitlement had not been removed by the introduction of the need for a claim to be made in 1985. It followed that the claimant could satisfy the conditions for entitlement in accordance with Regulation 10 of the ICA Regulation prior to her 65th birthday and was accordingly entitled to payment of that benefit from the time that she did claim (1993) though backdating was limited to one year.

**p. 168,** *annotations to section 71*

As with Attendance Allowance, DLA is payable under modified conditions to those who are terminally ill. (See note to section 66.) Section 72(5) provides that those who are terminally ill (*i.e.* not expected to live for more than 6 months) qualify for the care component of DLA at the highest rate, and do so immediately their terminal condition is identified without the need to satisfy the qualification period, and to be entitled for the remainder of their life. In *CDLA 1304/95* the Commissioner held that this applied to a child under 16 and that section 72(6), which requires demonstration of requirements substantially in excess of those required for a normal child of the same age, has no application to a case determined under subsection (5). In other words condition (b) and (c) of section 72(1) are deemed to be satisfied as a result of subsection (5), and the "under sixteens" test applies only to claimants qualifying by the ordinary routes.

This contrasts with a claim for the mobility component under section 73. There the equivalent provision for those who are terminally ill is section 73(9)(b), but in the same case the Commissioner points out that it removes only the necessity of satisfying a qualifying period—it remains necessary for the claimant to satisfy the "walking test" in the usual way and also to satisfy the extra requirements rule of the "under sixteen" test of subsection (4).

**pp. 196–199,** *annotations to section 94(1): "arising ... in the course of employment"*

Being assaulted at home by one's next door neighbour might be thought unlikely to constitute personal injury through accident arising out of and in the course of employment so as to dictate the granting of a declaration of industrial accident, thus opening the way to state-provided compensation for the disabling effects of injury suffered at and through work. That it can do so in some circumstances is made clear by Commissioner Goodman's decision in *CI/14111/1996* (starred as *7/97*). The case is valuable in showing, at the very least, that some of those vulnerable to assault because of their work (civil servants, social workers, police officers, teachers) may still be protected by the industrial injuries scheme against some of the disabling consequences even where the assault occurred away from work. But it also further highlights some of the anomalies created by maintaining a separate system of state compensation for injuries suffered at and through work.

Here the applicant for an industrial accident declaration was a Benefits Agency clerical worker who was assaulted on her drive, when at home on sick leave, by a neighbour (Mr O) for reasons clearly connected with and the product of her employment; she was assaulted because she was seen as a DSS spy who had reported the neighbour for claiming benefit whilst working. Until that point there had been no problems between the neighbours. The accident thus undoubtedly arose "out of the employment". The key issue was whether the accident arose in the course of her employment.

The AO decided not. The SSAT by a majority found in favour of the claimant on the basis that "because of her work, her home became equivalent to her place of employment at the time the assault occurred" (paragraph 8). The dissenting member thought that

> "the line between being in the course of employment or not had not been crossed: that as [the claimant] was at home off sick the circumstances were too remote from her employment to say the accident arose in the course of it. Further [the claimant] had said she reported Mr O both because of her loyalty to work but also as a member of the public" (paragraph 9)

Commissioner Goodman set aside the SSAT decision. While recognising that the reasons given showed "considerable thought", he pointed out that *Nancollas*, on which heavy reliance had been placed, had been overtaken as regards certain aspects by *Smith v. Stages*, a decision of the House of Lords. Moreover,

> "it also has to be remembered that, ultimately, a decision as to whether or not a person is 'in the course of' their employment is a decision on fact, though legal issues may arise as in this case" (paragraph 8).

The simple approach taken by the SSAT majority was incorrect. The claimant's position was not like that of a "police officer or fireman who may be on constant call even at home and therefore while at home can be regarded in the course of his employment" (paragraph 10). The Commissioner seemed attracted by the following approach in paragraph 12 of *RI(I)67/52:*

> "The definition of an industrial accident as one 'arising out of and in the course of' a person's employment means, briefly, an accident arising while he is doing what his contract obliges him to do, *and because of a risk created by what his contract obliges him to do*. The accident must, therefore, be one which happens while he is within what has been called *the scope or ambit* of his work" (cited in paragraph 7, emphasis supplied by Commissioner Goodman)

Commissioner Goodman saw two reasons for regarding the claimant as within the course of her employment, each of which causes some problems of application beyond the specific facts of the instant case, and each of which is apt to take matters into the types of areas of evidential difficulty that have grounded one reason for government refusal to extend the industrial injuries scheme to cover the self-employed. In this case, however, the facts were undisputed.

In the first place, had she not been at home sick on the day in question (a normal working day), she would have been at work in the office. The Commissioner then noted the reference to "employed earner's employment" in section 94(1) and the definition of "employed earner" in C & BA 1992, section 2. In *R(G)2/95* in the context of ICA, Commissioner Goodman held that someone on extended sick leave and in receipt of SSP and sick pay was absent "only with the consent and authority of the employer and subject to any qualifications to that authority" (paragraph 12 of *CI/14111/1996*). But he so held for the purposes of the earnings limit with respect to ICA, under a regulation then applicable which disregarded earnings of an employee absent from work with the consent of the employer. So there the earnings of the claimant when on sick leave were disregarded. Applying that to the industrial injuries context in *CI14111/1996* (starred as 7/97), Commissioner Goodman considered that this meant that whilst at home on sick leave the claimant remained serving under her contract of service and was still in employed earner's employment. Hence, because she was "forced to be at home because of illness and was at home only with the consent and authority of her employer" she could in Commissioner Goodman's judgement still be regarded when on authorised sick leave as in the course of her employment. As noted earlier, being then assaulted because of her work satisfied the "out of the employment" criterion so that her case fulfilled the requisites of section 94(1). It is submitted that, although Commissioner Goodman does not expressly so confine his principle, one can regard someone as only so protected in this way on normal working days and during normal working hours, and, of course, only against risks arising because of the employment itself and not against risks arising merely from being at home. So a work-related assault which took place at a weekend, or when on holiday at home, would presumably not be covered. Nor, presumably, would falling down the stairs at home during normal working hours while on authorised sick leave; on general principle the work connection is absent but s.101 might apply. Nor presumably would the protection of the industrial injuries scheme extend to someone with a fixed workplace (*e.g.* a schoolteacher) assaulted on the way home from school or when out shopping; in such cases the work-related nature of the assault (if proven) satisfies the "out of" criterion, but applying the general principles of the "what, when and where" test, neither can properly be said to arise "in the course of employment", the individual in each instance both being back in the public domain and beyond the control of the employer. But all these examples as much stress the anomalies and difficulties of line-drawing on an acceptable basis, arising from a separate system of compensation for accidents happening at and because of work, as suggest that Commissioner Goodman's extension of the workplace to the situation before him was necessarily wrong in principle. It will be interesting to see whether the majority of Commissioners express agreement with the approach to workers on authorised sick leave when the decision is circulated to them for consideration as to whether it warrants reporting. If it is not reported, the problem will then be one of guessing whether that is because the majority of his colleagues disagree with him or whether it is thought that the approach taken is so inherent in accepted general principle as not to warrant reporting, adding nothing to the existing *corpus* of law on the subject. But it is surely arguable that while it may be true to say that the claimant is still in employment with or employed by her employee when on sick leave, it does not necessarily follow that she is in the course of her employment; surely for that it depends on what she was doing. Moreover if Commissioner Goodman is right on the point, then, given the width of section

101 (main volume pages 205–206), deeming a range of situations arising in the course of employment also to arise out of it where on general principles they might not do so, the claimant at home sick who suffers injury when falling over the dog thus suffers personal injury through accident arising out of and in the course of employed earner's employment. Surely that cannot be right? Commissioner Goodman did not appear to be saying that only because this case arose out of the employment in a direct sense, could it be held to also arise in the course of it. But perhaps in principle that is the way the case ought to be confined if further anomalies and peculiarities are to be avoided.

The second reason advanced by Commissioner Goodman for holding that the accident befell the claimant in the course of her employment is undoubtedly correct in terms of general principle, but one which it is not easy to see fulfilled in the particular case before him on the facts as given in the report. Commissioner Goodman noted:

> "At the hearing before me, [the claimant] gave evidence that she had to do 'preparation work' at home and was credited by the Benefits Agency under their 'flexitime' system for the hours she spent at home doing that work. That evidence was not, I think, before the tribunal. It does, however, mean that *ad hoc* her home could, indeed, become her place of work . . ." (paragraph 13).

That is of course correct as a matter of general principle, and offers some aid and comfort to those so required to work at home who suffer injury in and through doing it. But this claimant was on authorised sick leave and walking down her drive when assaulted, so it is unclear how it applied to her, unless she had taken a "reasonably incidental" short break from doing such preparatory work. But establishing when a claimant was doing such work and what departures from it are also covered takes one into the sorts of areas of evidential difficulty and demarcation that have caused successive governments to refuse to extend the coverage of the industrial injuries compensation scheme to the self-employed.

**p. 212,** *section 113*

A modified reciprocal agreement with the United States of America has been concluded which comes into force on September 1, 1997. See The Social Security (United States of America) Order 1997 (S.I. 1997 No. 1778).

**p. 221,** *annotations to section 142*

Decision *CF/12/94* is now reported as *R(F)2/95*.

**pp. 267–268,** *"gives up regular employment": the effect of the new regulation 3*

This regulation came into force on March 24, 1996, the date on which it was inserted by the Social Security (Industrial Injuries and Diseases)(Miscellaneous Amendment) Regulations 1996. In decisions *CI094/94* and *CI600/94* (starred together as *46/96*), Commissioner Howell held that it removed entitlement to REA and replaced it with retirement allowance for life with effect from March

31, 1996 (the beginning of the week after March 24, 1996) even in the case of two ladies who had attained pensionable age prior to March 24 and had in normal parlance given up (but not retired from) regular employment because of incapacity long before either April 10, 1989 (the date in C & BA 1992, Sched. 7, para. 13(1)) or March 24, 1996 (the date regulation 3 came into force). The two ladies would not otherwise have been deprived of REA by para. 13(1) because of the fact that they had as at October 1, 1989 been long out of work so that they could not be said to have "given up" regular employment on any day on or after that date as paragraph 13(1)(b) as supplemented by the original 1990 regulations required, "gives up" bearing its ordinary natural meaning (*R(I)2/93, R(I)3/93*). Regulation 3 did, however, deprive them of it and transfer them to retirement allowance by, albeit artificially, regarding them as having given it up. See in particular paragraphs 37, 38 and 40–49. Note, however, that leave to appeal to the Court of Appeal was granted on September 8, 1997.

The case is very useful in charting the bumpy and twisting path of attempts to make entitlement to REA cease on retirement, and makes clear that regulation 3 is *intra vires* the rule making power in C & BA, paragraph 13(8).

Since both ladies had attained the age of 65 before the regulation deprived them of REA, the condition linked to pensionable age in paragraph 13(1) had no discriminatory effect, rendering it unnecessary in their case to consider any possible application of Council Directive 79/7 EEC (main volume, pages 374–378). A number of test cases in which discrimination contrary to the Directive is a very real issue are pending before the Commissioners and in July 1997 directions were given in respect of them by Commissioner Howell that they be listed for oral hearing at the earliest possible date (*CI6608/96, CI537/97, CI1847/97, CI1896/97*).

**p. 358,** *annotation to section 29: pilot schemes*

See further the following set of regulations: the Jobseeker's Allowance (Contract for Work) Regulations 1997 (S.I. 1997 No. 982); the Jobseeker's Allowance (Project Work Pilot Scheme) Regulations 1997 (S.I. 1997 No. 983); the Jobseeker's Allowance (Workskill Courses) Pilot (No. 2) Regulations 1997 (S.I. 1997 No. 1909).

# EUROPEAN COMMUNITY LAW

**p. 376,** *annotations to Article 7*

See *R(P)1/96*.

# REGULATIONS

**p. 426,** *annotations to regulation 24*

Changes made to the Adjudication Regulations with effect from April 28, 1997, reflected in the new text above, omitted reference to the possibility of an appellant requesting leave to appeal to the Commissioner at the hearing once the decision was announced. Since such applications must now be made in accordance with regulation 3 and Schedule 2, it follows that such applications must be made in writing and can no longer be made orally at the end of a hearing.

**p. 436,** *regulation 67A*

With effect from August 25, 1997, a new regulation 67A is added as follows:

### "Review in attendance allowance and disability living allowance cases

67A.—(1) Failure by a person to attend for, or submit to, a medical examination under the provisions made under section 57A of the Administration Act (medical examinations) is prescribed as a relevant change of circumstances for the purposes of section 30(2)(b) or 35(1)(b) of the Administration Act (review on the grounds of relevant change of circumstances). (2) In the case where an award of attendance or disability living allowance falls to be reviewed under section 30(2)(b) or 35(1)(b) of the Administration Act (review on the grounds of relevant change of circumstances) in the circumstances prescribed under paragraph (1), the decision given on review shall have effect from the date determined by the Secretary of State under regulation 8D(1) of the Social Security (Attendance Allowance) Regulations 1991 or regulation 5B(1) of the Social Security (Disability Living Allowance) Regulations 1991, as the case may be."

**p. 440,** *amending regulations*

Add to the list of amending regulations:
The Social Security (Attendance Allowance and Disability Living Allowance)(Miscellaneous Amendments) Regulations 1997 (S.I. 1997 No. 1839).

**p. 622,** *President's Circulars*

The President has issued revisions to Circulars, 1, 2, 4 and 9, and issued a new Circular No. 13. There follows a current list of circulars and full copies of the amended circulars and of the new circular.

# PRESIDENT'S CIRCULARS

### INDEX

|  |  | **Date** |
|---|---|---|
| No. 1 | Adjournments | *Amended June 1997* |
| No. 2 | Recording and notifying tribunal proceedings and decisions: form and content | *Amended June 1997* |
| No. 3 | No smoking policy | October 1995 |
| No. 4 | Domiciliary hearings | *Amended June 1997* |
| No. 5 | [withdrawn March 1995] |  |
| No. 6 | Setting-aside applications: conduct of tribunal chairmen/members/assessors/ITS staff | October 1995 |
| No. 7 | Tribunals' use of "Liberty to Restore" | October 1995 |
| No. 8 | The admission of late appeals | *Withdrawn April 1996* |
| No. 9 | Action in multiple cases where the decision of a commissioner or of a superior court is awaited | June 1997 |
| No. 10 | Correcting accidental errors in tribunal decisions | *Amended September 1996* |
| No. 11 | Confidentiality in Child Support Appeal Tribunals | *Amended June 1997* [not reproduced] |
| No. 12 | References to the Court of Justice of the European Communities [ECJ] | November 1996 |
| No. 13 | The obtaining of further medical evidence [all jurisdictions] by order of the tribunal | June 1997 |

# PRESIDENT'S CIRCULAR NO. 1

## ADJOURNMENTS

*Generally*

1. Tribunals have the power to adjourn hearings, either of their own motion or upon application of a party and it will often be necessary for the tribunal, in the interests of justice, to exercise that power.

2. Tribunals should, however, remind themselves that the unnecessary adjournment of a hearing should always be avoided; the consequent delay can cause hardship or distress to a party, and can waste valuable public resources which could be more efficiently and properly used.

3. Tribunals will wish, therefore, to articulate very carefully the reason for an adjournment before initiating or agreeing to that action, and to be sure, in those cases where the seeking or obtaining of additional evidence [medical or otherwise] is the reason for the adjournment, that that additional evidence is likely to be available without unreasonable delay, is likely to assist the tribunal in its deliberations and is relevant to the issue to be decided.

4. I regard it as good practice in the fulfilment of the judicial role to articulate the reason for the adjournment in the written decision, and I would hope that tribunal chairmen would follow that practice. An entry reading simply "adjourned for additional evidence", I would not regard as meeting that criterion of good judicial practice. A form now exists [ITS/ADJ] which is to be used on every occasion when a tribunal adjourns a hearing and which is to be handed to the parties who are present before the tribunal or sent within two days of the hearing to any absent party.

*Where the tribunal accepts that it needs further evidence*

5. The tribunal's judicial task is to determine an appeal before it, on the basis of its assessment of the evidence produced, its findings of fact following such assessment and its application of the relevant law to those findings. Experience shows that in the normal course of events the evidence produced is such as to enable the tribunal properly to complete this task without an adjournment for the purpose of producing further evidence.

6. However, there may be circumstances where the available evidence is insufficient so that it is in the interests of justice for the tribunal to exercise its discretion to adjourn.

7. It is important for the adjournment decision to record who should supply any further evidence, *i.e.* the appellant, his representative or the AO and by when it should be supplied; it is also important to impose a timescale for the case to be relisted. The direction should always make it clear whether the case is to be listed before the same or a differently constituted tribunal. The reservation of cases to the same tribunal should only be done in exceptional circumstances, *i.e.* where substantial oral evidence has been taken or complex legal argument is under consideration.

8. If the tribunal is exercising its power under section 53 of the Social Security Administration Act 1992 so that the ITS is required to take some action that exercise of power should be expressly indicated on the form ITS [ADJ] and attention should be drawn to the need for the ITS administration to take relevant action and to the form which that action should take.

9. Where the tribunal adjourns for the ITS to obtain a medical report it is important that the report is obtained expeditiously, so that the matter can be relisted without unnecessary delay. There is, therefore, a need to publicise the ways in which the tribunal's decision to adjourn to obtain a medical report may be formulated in such a way as to minimise any such delay.

10. As a first step the form ITS/ADJ on which the chairman records the tribunal's decision to adjourn, should clearly summarise the reasons why the tribunal considered that it should adjourn and why it considered that the ITS should obtain a medical report. Form ITS/FME 1 should be contemporaneously completed in all such cases. The purpose of the form is to specify the kind of report being sought, from whom, whether it requires fresh examination or review of existing medical records, what aspects of the claimed benefit it addresses and to what questions such as diagnosis or treatment, it should be directed. This information is essential to enable the formulation of a proper request for a medical report.

11. It is the chairman's responsibility to complete ITS/FME1, which should be done in the hearing room and in the presence of any party who has attended the hearing so that a medical member of the tribunal or the medical assessor can advise upon its content. The use of form DAT 32 is now discontinued.

*Further considerations*

12. Tribunals should always remind themselves that where benefit has been withdrawn upon review, the burden of providing that that action was justified, upon the balance of probabilities, lies upon the AO. Where the tribunal is of the opinion that the AO should have sought medical or other evidence to put before the tribunal in order to discharge that burden, but has failed to do so without good cause, the tribunal will always want to ask itself [albeit recognising that they exercise an inquisitorial jurisdiction] whether the tribunal should expend resources in and cause further delay by seeking evidence which the AO should have obtained in order to support the review decision. The preferable course may be either to adjourn to enable the AO to seek the necessary evidence within a specified timescale [if a just decision cannot be reached without that evidence and if the PO can offer an acceptable explanation for the failure to produce it] or to decide the case by reference to the facts before the tribunal and the applicable burden of proof.

13. A similar problem may arise where an appellant, on first application for the benefit, appeals against the disallowance, produces no medical evidence yet suggests that it is available and that the tribunal should seek it. It may also occur that, during the course of the hearing, the tribunal identifies a need for additional medical evidence. Tribunals should remind themselves that in these cases the burden of proof lies with the appellant [also on the balance of probabilities] and that they should then consider the extent to which public resources should be expended if what is then proposed is the seeking of evidence which, strictly, the appellant should have sought and produced before the hearing. That consideration may not be appropriate where the tribunal itself identifies the need for further evidence. In deciding whether or not to adjourn and, if so, for what

purpose, tribunals should, while reminding themselves that they exercise an inquisitorial jurisdiction, consider the likely availability of the suggested evidence within a reasonable timescale, its relevance to the issues before the tribunal and [where appropriate] the appellant's reasons for not providing that evidence to the tribunal. If the tribunal decides to adjourn for evidence to be obtained, the adjournment decision should make it clear whether the ITS or the appellant is to obtain the evidence and should impose realistic timescales for evidence provision and relisting of the hearing.

9. The practical directions for the obtaining of medical reports and other medical evidence are contained in President's Circular No. 13.

JUNE 1997         HIS HONOUR JUDGE KEITH BASSINGTHWAIGHTE
                                                    PRESIDENT

## PRESIDENT'S CIRCULAR NO. 2

## RECORDING AND NOTIFYING TRIBUNAL PROCEEDINGS AND DECISIONS: FORM AND CONTENT

1. *Record of proceedings*

In this area amendments occurred by virtue of the Social Security [Adjudication] and Child Support Amendment Regulations 1996 which came into force on February 28, 1996. As a result of those regulations, chairmen should keep a written record of evidence [both oral and written], submissions and the progress of the hearing [a "record of proceedings"] on form ITS[RP]; that record will be kept for 18 months and supplied in its handwritten form to any party to the proceedings who requests them.

2. Chairmen are reminded that the presence of the regulation does not mean that the record of proceedings should never be issued. It is a chairman's decision whether to do so and he/she might consider it prudent [and a saving of administrative resources] to request that a copy of that record be supplied in particularly contentious cases where an appeal—and a request for a copy of the record of proceedings—is likely. If that is done, the full decision [see paragraph 12 below] should record that a copy of the manuscript note of proceedings on form ITS[RP] is attached.

3. *Oral notification*

Whenever an appellant or his/her representative attends a tribunal hearing, I regard it as good judicial practice and in the interests of the appellant for a tribunal chairman orally to announce the result at the conclusion of the hearing, unless there are compelling reasons to the contrary. This applies whatever the nature of the tribunal's decision.

4. The following are examples of "compelling reasons":
   (a) An appellant/representative does not or cannot wait to hear the decision.
   (b) An appellant/representative cannot hear or understand the decision.
   (c) There is reason to believe that, if told the decision, a party will become distressed or distraught.
   (d) There is reason to believe that a party will become violent to himself or another, or to property, if told the decision at the conclusion of the hearing.
   (e) The decision is too complex to explain to a party without causing undue confusion or anxiety.

5. The chairman should normally use non-technical ordinary language to indicate the decision and its effect, and should explain the procedures for written notification.

6. *Written notification*

As a result of further Adjudication Regulation changes following the enactment of Statutory Instrument 1996 No. 2450, new written decision procedures come into effect on and from 21 October 1996. The new procedures apply to SSATs,

MATs, DATs and CSATs but not to VDTs. The Adjudication Regulations provided, inter alia, for the introduction of decision notices on the day of the hearing and for statements of the tribunal's findings of fact and reasons for its decision to be provided later, either on request or of a chairman's own motion. In this Circular, the latter document is referred to, for convenience, as a "full decision".

7. *Decision Notices.* A decision notice is a form which the regulation gives me the power to approve. I have approved a form of decision notice for use in each jurisdiction to be known respectively as ITS[DN] [SSAT], [CSAT] etc.; only that form as drafted has my approval under the Adjudication Regulations. That printed form should not be amended nor should anything [other than an AWT schedule] be attached to it. The decision notice is to be legibly handwritten by the chairman; the tribunal clerk will hand a copy of the carbonised decision notice to the parties as they leave the hearing. They will, either at the same time or earlier, have been advised in writing of their right to appeal and to apply for a record of proceedings and a full decision, but tribunal chairmen may want specifically to enquire of the parties whether they want a full decision, since the earlier such a request is notified, the less the effort expended in producing it. The decision notice dispenses with the need for separate forms AT3A or DAT28A [the use of which has been discontinued].

8. *Decision notices must be written and issued in every case and at the hearing where the decision has been announced.* If the decision has not been announced or following determination of a case in the absence of a party or by consideration of the papers alone, the decision notice should be written by the chairman who was not present at the hearing on the next working day following the hearing. The decision notice will record the decision of the tribunal [in sufficient detail, where an appellant is successful, to enable immediate payment of benefit] and will provide for inclusion of a summary of the tribunal's reasons for that decision [see paragraph 9, below].

9. Where there has been no request for a full decision at the hearing and the chairman does not intend to issue one, the decision notice will contain a summary of the tribunal's reasons for its decision: that summary is not intended to be an exhaustive recital of the tribunal's process of reasoning but to be a two or three sentence explanation of the reasons for success or failure. For example, in an IB case, the relevant paragraph could read "After examining all the claimed and relevant descriptor areas, we were satisfied that the appellant could not be awarded sufficient points to reach the AWT threshold of 15" or "After examining all the claimed and relevant descriptor areas, the appellant satisfied the AWT as a result of our award of points with reference to the following physical functions i.e. walking [7 points], standing [7 points] and hearing [8 points]." Where a full decision is to be issued or where an extempore decision has been given and taped, the relevant paragraph of the decision notice could read "A written document, which includes the reasons for our decision, will be issued to the parties later" or "The reasons for our decision were explained to the parties at the hearing."

10. There are two decision notices for use in DATs: the ITS[DAT] [REF] and the ITS[DAT] [AW], the former recording a refusal, the latter an award. In those cases where the award of both care and mobility components of DLA are in issue, but the tribunal awards one and not the other, chairmen should be aware that both decision notices should be issued.

11. It is always for a chairman to decide whether only a decision notice, or a decision notice and full decision, needs to be issued in any particular case.

He/she should always consider very carefully to what extent the decision notice alone is appropriate for the case which the tribunal has just decided, bearing in mind the area and scope of dispute, and the likelihood of appeal.

12. There may be some cases which are so straightforward that, even if requested to provide a full decision, the chairman will not be able to add anything to what is contained in the decision notice. Where that is the case, the decision notice should clearly state on its face that it "includes the full statement of the reasons for the tribunal's decision and of its findings on questions of fact material thereto to which Regulation 23[3A] of the Social Security [Adjudication] Regulations 1995 refers".

13. *Full Decisions.* A chairman will need to prepare a decision which contains "the reasons for the tribunal's decision and its findings on questions of fact material thereto" only if he/she decides to do so or if a party, either at the hearing or within 21 days of issue of a decision notice, so requests. Chairmen will note that the full decision incorporates, by specific reference therein, the terms of the decision notice already issued.

14. If a chairman wishes to give a full decision at the hearing, the regulations provide that he/she may choose to deliver an extempore decision which can be tape-recorded. If a chairman chooses that option and if a request is made for a transcript of that record, it will be typed and sent to the chairman for signature. *It will not be possible for the chairman to correct or alter the typed transcript, except in the case of typing errors.*

15. If a chairman decides upon, or a party requests, preparation of a full decision at the hearing, I would expect it to be ordinarily available within 14 days of the hearing. Chairmen may use any of the currently approved methods for preparation of that decision and should ensure that the decision is provided to the ITS office concerned within three working days. The chairman should ensure, whenever a clerk is not present in the tribunal room to appreciate that a full decision will be issued, that the clerk is so advised; the intention to issue a full decision should also be apparent from the fact of the decision notice [see paragraph 9, above].

16. If a party requests preparation of a full decision within 21 days of the issue of the decision notice, the chairman concerned must be notified of that request within three days of its receipt in ITS offices and he/she must be sent, within that same timescale, a copy of the tribunal papers [and of any additional written evidence received thereat], of the record of proceedings and of the decision notice. Chairmen should aim to provide that full decision to the ITS office within three working days of receipt of the request. I consider that a chairman may, at his/her discretion, agree to issue a full decision even though the request is made outside the 21 day period. If such a request is made, but refused, I do not, however, consider that a chairman is obliged to give reasons for that decision.

17. Chairmen will no doubt wish to keep some personal record of the identities of those present at the hearing and of the rationale of decisions and closed session discussion against the possibility that a full decision may be later requested. For that reason, judicial notebooks have been acquired and will be available to all chairmen. They are personal records to be kept by chairmen and are *not* to be deposited in ITS offices for safekeeping; it should be noted that it is my opinion that these notebooks will not contain formal records, the production of which I would expect to be compellable either by parties or by the appellate jurisdictions.

18. *I regret that ITS resources cannot be used for the precautionary recording of full decisions simply in case one should later be requested.* Clerks have, therefore, been advised to decline the use of ITS recording equipment unless it is indicated in the decision notice that a full decision will be issued or the chairman, having initially decided not to issue a full decision, changes his/her mind on the day of the hearing and so advises the clerk. If chairmen wish to do so on their own equipment, that is a matter for them but it would obviously assist if it was ensured that that equipment is compatible with that in use in ITS offices.

19. The issue of a decision notice does not affect rights of appeal against the tribunal's decision. Time limits for appeal now run from the date of issue of the full decision.

JUNE 1997   HIS HONOUR JUDGE KEITH BASSINGTHWAIGHTE
PRESIDENT

# PRESIDENT'S CIRCULAR NO. 4

## DOMICILIARY HEARINGS

1. Tribunals have the power to hold a hearing at a claimant's home in appropriate cases: they are known as domiciliary visits [DVs]. A tribunal is never under a legal obligation to hold such a hearing.

2. Administrative staff of the ITS are not to arrange a DV before the tribunal has convened to hear the case, unless the President, a regional or any full-time chairman has so instructed. That instruction will generally not be given unless it is obvious that there are no other reasonable means of ensuring that a just decision is made by the tribunal, taking into account the principles of natural justice.

3. A tribunal or chairman should always give very careful consideration to the facts before directing a DV. In particular, consider whether:
   (a) there is already sufficient evidence on which to allow an appeal in full,
   (b) sufficient evidence to reach a just decision can reasonably be obtained in some other way, including those indicated in paragraph 4 below, and
   (c) there is any other reasonable way to obtain the attendance of the parties, including those indicated in paragraph 5 below.

4. "Other ways of obtaining evidence" include:
   (a) requesting the attendance of a family member, a carer or some other witness who could give the evidence that could be given by the parties;
   (b) requesting written or recorded evidence from the parties, a carer or some other witness;
   (c) referring a question of special difficulty to an expert [including a general practitioner] for report under section 53 of the Social Security Administration Act 1993;
   (d) the exercise of the power of the chairman to give such directions as he may consider necessary or desirable for just, effective and efficient conduct of the proceedings under Regulation 2[1] [aa] of S.I. 1996 No. 2450.

5. "Other ways of obtaining the attendance of the parties" include:
   (a) providing a taxi or a private hire care to bring the parties from home to the tribunal hearing, and
   (b) arranging for the parties to be brought from home to the usual venue by St John's Ambulance or similar suitable vehicle.

6. In deciding whether to adjourn and order a DV, a tribunal, in particular, should also take into account:
   (a) that members of the tribunal may have disabilities which would cause difficulties in arranging a DV, and
   (b) that it may often be preferable to adjourn for another hearing at the usual venue, rather than to arrange an unnecessary DV.

7. There may be occasions when only the obtaining of a General Practitioner's report will enable a tribunal or chairman to make an informed

decision. Provided that unacceptable delay will not be occasioned by such a request, such a report may be requested before a tribunal or chairman makes the decision.

JUNE 1997   HIS HONOUR JUDGE KEITH BASSINGTHWAIGHTE
PRESIDENT

# PRESIDENT'S CIRCULAR NO. 9

## ACTION IN MULTIPLE CASES WHERE THE DECISION OF A COMMISSIONER OR OF A SUPERIOR COURT IS AWAITED

1. Where these cases are concerned, [which are referred to generically as "appeal dependent cases"] it is always necessary to consider the best way of dealing with them. On many occasions, I will agree that it is desirable that they should not be listed for hearing until the decision in the lead case is known.

2. Where that action has been taken, appellants and their representatives will have been informed of the reason for that action in the terms of the specimen letter attached, and will also have been informed of their right to require a case to be listed despite my direction to the contrary.

3. Such cases may, therefore, come before a tribunal. If that occurs, tribunals will have before them a copy of the ITS letter to the appellant/representative and of any additional information, giving the full context of the case and its likely progress through the appellate levels beyond the ITS. It will then be necessary for the tribunal to decide whether to hear the case or to adjourn it, pending resolution of the relevant issue[s].

4. Tribunals should ensure that they are in possession of all such additional information before making a decision. They must make that decision judicially on the facts before them, having considered the submissions of the presenting officer and/or the appellant and his/her representative.

5. Tribunals should bear in mind that, although delay will occur if there is an adjournment:
   (a) a successful appellant [if the case had been heard] is likely to have gained little, since the Secretary of State may well appeal the tribunal's decision, which will permit the suspension of payment of any awarded benefit in such disputed circumstances, and
   (b) all benefit routes are not closed to an appellant who alleges that he/she suffers financial hardship as a result of the delay in resolution of the appeal.

6. It sometimes occurs that a party or representative before the tribunal will allege that "there is a lead case pending", although the tribunal has no information before it of the type mentioned in the preceding paragraphs. Tribunals should be wary of acting upon unsubstantiated suggestion and should, unless compelling detail is provided and if there is sufficient information and evidence before it, decide the case according to the existing law.

JUNE 1997         HIS HONOUR JUDGE KEITH BASSINGTHWAIGHTE
                                                PRESIDENT

## SPECIMEN LETTER

Dear

IMPORTANT INFORMATION ABOUT YOUR APPEAL

1. I am writing about your appeal against *[here describe the nature of the appeal]*.

2. Your appeal, with many others, involves a difficult point of law. *[Here describe the legal issue]*. Consequently, *[here describe who has appealed, to which court and the time frame for appeal]*. Until then, therefore, the law is not clear or settled.

3. If your case was to come before a tribunal and be decided in your favour, I understand that the Adjudication Officer is likely to appeal that decision to the Commissioners. Any advantage you may have gained as a result of the decision could then be lost, since, pending the appeal in your case being decided by the Commissioner, the Secretary of State has, by law, the power to suspend payment of any benefit awarded by the tribunal. In view of that, and of the number of similar cases, a great deal of time and energy could be wasted with little positive outcome for any of the parties. For this reason, we consider that it is in the interests of all concerned not to hear your case—or that of any of the other similar placed appellants—until this period of uncertainty is resolved by the decision of the *[here insert identity of appeal court]*. You have my assurance that your appeal will then be dealt with urgently.

4. I appreciate that this letter may come as a disappointment to you. However, I hope that you will accept our concern about delays which arise when difficult questions have to be resolved in the Courts.

5. I will keep you informed from time to time about how the lead appeal is progressing. However, it may be some months before I have any new information to report. You should be aware that if you disagree with the decision not to list your case for hearing for the present, you can request the Independent Tribunal Service [ITS] to list it for hearing. If you do, I am informed that the department's representative is likely to apply for an adjournment; if that is granted by the tribunal, it means that resources have been used which could have been applied to the determination of other cases not affected by pending legislation. I hope, therefore, that you will agree that the decision taken is in the best interests of all concerned.

6. It may also help you to know that not all benefit routes are closed to you while the legal issue is going through the Courts. You should contact your local office of the Benefits Agency for advice or seek that advice from representative sources, such as the Citizens' Advice Bureau or a local welfare rights' organisation. The Secretary of State does also have the discretion to decide not to suspend any benefit which may be awarded by a tribunal if hardship is caused by that suspension. You may, therefore, use that argument if you ask for your case to be listed, despite this letter, and if the Department's representative seeks to persuade the tribunal to adjourn your application. You should realise, however, that the discretion has only been exercised in severe cases in the recent past.

7. I am sending a copy of this letter to major representatives' organisations, although not necessarily to individual representatives. Any enquiries should be addressed to this office.

Yours sincerely,

## PRESIDENT'S CIRCULAR NO. 13

### THE OBTAINING OF FURTHER MEDICAL EVIDENCE [ALL JURISDICTIONS] BY ORDER OF THE TRIBUNAL

1. The ITS has now introduced new procedures where a tribunal decides that the ITS should obtain further medical evidence following an adjournment of an appeal. Requests for medical reports will be actioned by the ITS administrative staff [not BAMS/DBC as was previously the case] and issued direct to the medical profession. Requests for Examining Medical Practitioner [EMP] reports in DATs and Hospital Case Notes' [HCNs] extracts in MATs will, in the future, be processed by the ITS administration via a medical services' contract with the private sector [these requests are still currently being processed via BAMS until the new contract is in place, however administrative staff will prepare the request before issuing to BAMS/DBC].

2. Further changes are as follows:
   (a) *Form DAT 32*—this is now obsolete,
   (b) *Introduction of form ITS/FME 1*—this form should be used in all jurisdictions when FME is required in the form of:
       Examining Medical Practitioner [EMP] reports
       GP factual reports
       Hospital factual reports
       Consultant reports
       Any other specialist reports, for example, school reports, and
   (c) It is the chairman's responsibility to complete the ITS/FME1, which should be done in the hearing room and in the presence of any party who has attended the hearing so that the medical member/assessor of the tribunal can advise upon the content of the questions to be addressed.

3. Tribunals should remind themselves, in the interests of a prompt resolution of an appeal, that GP factual and EMP reports can usually be received within four weeks, whereas other reports can often take several months to obtain.

4. *Referrals back to BAMS for the All Work Test [AWT] [IB cases only]*. AWT referrals should continue to be requested in the usual way on the ITS/DN/ADJ. Administrative staff will continue to forward these requests to the originating Benefit Agency [BA] office as is currently the case.

5. *X-rays* [MAT cases only]. Form MAT 5 series should continue to be used and requests issued directly to the owner of the x-rays. Requests for new x-rays will also continue to be processed in the usual way.

6. *Hospital Case Notes* [MAT cases only]. Sight of the original case notes can be requested where needed but tribunals should always consider very carefully whether those notes are needed. It is the case that notes of treatment at the time of injury will not always be helpful. MATs are often concerned not with the treatment of the injury but with the resultant disablement, which they have to assess. If production of HCNs is considered relevant, wherever possible an extract of HCNs should be requested, as suggested in my memorandum of April 1, 1997 [a copy of which is attached to this Circular]. These requests

should be made on the ITS/DN/ADJ. Another alternative to sight of the HCNs is the hospital factual report, see paragraph 2b above.

JUNE 1997　　　HIS HONOUR JUDGE KEITH BASSINGTHWAIGHTE
　　　　　　　　　　　　　　　　　　　　　　　THE PRESIDENT

ENCL:

## MEMORANDUM

| | |
|---|---|
| From: | THE PRESIDENT |
| To: | ALL FULL-TIME CHAIRMEN |
| | MAT AND DAT PART-TIME CHAIRMEN |
| CC: | REGIONAL CHAIRMEN |
| | CHIEF EXECUTIVE |

References: 25/10/1, 25/24/1

### REQUESTS FOR HOSPITAL CASE NOTES [HCNs]

1. As you will by now be aware, the ITS is changing the procedures for requesting further medical evidence. Historically, all requests for further medical evidence [FME] have been processed by the Benefits Agency Medical Service [BAMs]. From April 1, 1997 the ITS takes responsibility for processing requests for FME with the exception of Examining Medical Practitioner [EMP] reports in DAT cases only and HCNs in MAT cases only. EMPs and HCNs will be processed via a medical services' contract with the private sector.

2. It is on the subject of HCN requests that I write to you now. It is recognised that on some occasions the MAT consider that reference to HCNs is essential in determining an appeal. Unless the tribunal specifically request that the actual HCNs are put before them, BAMS request the HCNs and prepare an extract of the notes which are relevant to the medical issues before the tribunal. Experience within the ITS suggests that the tribunal's needs are normally met by this procedure.

3. Under the terms of the new contract the contractor will only provide the ITS with an extract of the case notes.

4. Where the tribunal request sight of the actual HCNs these will be requested by the ITS direct from the hospital concerned, but this is not without problems for the ITS. The two main problems are:
   (a) that the HCNs are provided to the ITS by the hospital under an arrangement which provides for their return to the hospital within 10 days. If this arrangement is not honoured by the ITS, the hospital has the right to withdraw the loan facility from the DSS in general, and
   (b) that the ITS would be responsible for the safe custody of HCNs. Should the ITS lose HCNs within its possession, it could find itself involved in significant and costly liability.

5. While, for the reasons mentioned above, I would wish you to consider carefully whether original HCNs are necessary rather than extracts from HCNs,

I would, of course, wish to make it plain that the decision to obtain an extract or production of the original HCN is purely a matter for the tribunal's judicial discretion.

6. These arrangements and the wider topic of medical evidence generally will be confirmed shortly in a President's Instruction.

1 April 1997

**p. 644,** *annotations to regulation 7*

Two further unreported Commissioner's decisions confirm the view that title to benefit cannot be gained when fees initially paid by a local authority have to be reimbursed by the claimant. In *CA/11185/1995* it was held that regulation 8(6) cannot be satisfied retrospectively. In both that decision and *CA/7126/1995* it was also held that regulation 59(4) of Adjudication Regulations precludes a subsequent claim to Attendance Allowance.

**p. 647,** *regulations 8C, 8D, 8E*

With effect from August 25, 1997 add regulations 8C, 8D, and 8E as follows:

**Medical examination in prescribed circumstances**

**8C.**—(1) The prescribed circumstances in which a person who is awarded attendance allowance shall be required to attend for, or submit himself to, a medical examination, are where the Secretary of State is undertaking an investigation under section 30(7A) of the Social Security Administration Act 1992.

(2) An examination under paragraph (1) shall be conducted by a medical practitioner who is—
  (a) approved by the Secretary of State; or
  (b) engaged by an organisation approved by the Secretary of State.

**Withholding of benefit in prescribed circumstances**

**8D.**—(1) Subject to paragraph (2), where a person who is receiving attendance allowance is required by the Secretary of State to attend for, or submit to, a medical examination under regulation 8C and fails to comply with that requirement on more than one occasion, that allowance may be withheld, in whole or in part, from a date, not earlier than the second occasion, as the Secretary of State shall determine.

(2) Paragraph (1) shall not apply where—
  (a) a person who is required to attend for, or submit to, a medical examination proves to the satisfaction of the Secretary of State that he has good cause for failing to comply with the requirement to attend for, or submit himself to, medical examination;
  (b) a person who is required to attend for, or submit to, a medical examination produces such evidence as is acceptable to the Secretary of State in place of a medical examination; or
  (c) the Secretary of State otherwise has available to him such evidence as is acceptable to him.

(3) For the purposes of paragraph (2)(a), the matters which are to be taken into account in determining whether a person has good cause shall include—
   (a) whether he was outside Great Britain at the relevant time;
   (b) his state of health at the relevant time; and
   (c) the nature of any disability from which he suffers.

**Payment of withheld benefit**
   8E.—(1) Where the Secretary of State is satisfied that no question arises in connection with his investigation referred to in regulation 8C(1), payment of the amount withheld and the attendance allowance shall be made forthwith.
   (2) Where a question arose in connection with an investigation referred to in regulation 8C(1) in respect of which—
   (a) the Secretary of State made an application for the review of a person's entitlement to attendance allowance under section 30 of the Social Security Administration Act 1992; and
   (b) an adjudication officer has made a determination;
payment of the attendance allowance shall be made in accordance with the adjudication officer's determination, on review, of the person's entitlement.
   (3) Where paragraph (1) or (2) does not apply and attendance allowance is withheld under regulation 8D for a period of more than 3 months, the Secretary of State shall—
   (a) make, with a view to review, an application to the adjudication officer on the ground that the person failed to attend for, or submit himself to, medical examination; and
   (b) make such payments as are determined, on review, by the adjudication officer.

**p. 649,** *Add to the list of amending and revoking regulations:*

Social Security (Attendance Allowance and Disability Living Allowance) (Miscellaneous Amendments) Regulations 1997 (S.I. 1997 No. 1839).

**p. 654,** *regulations 5A, 5B, 5C.*

With effect from August 25, 1997 add regulations 5A, 5B and 5C as follows.

**"Medical examination in prescribed circumstances**
   5A.—(1) The prescribed circumstances in which a person who is awarded disability living allowance shall be required to attend for, or submit himself to, a medical examination, are where the Secretary of State is undertaking an investigation under section 30(7A) of the Administration Act
   (2) An examination under paragraph (1) shall be conducted by a medical practitioner who is—
   (a) approved by the Secretary of State; or
   (b) engaged by an organisation approved by the Secretary of State.

## Withholding of benefit in prescribed circumstances
**5B.—**

(1) Subject to paragraph (2), where a person who is receiving disability living allowance is required by the Secretary of State, to attend for, or submit to, a medical examination under regulation 5A and fails to comply with that requirement on more than one occasion, that allowance may be withheld, in whole or in part, from a date, not earlier than the second occasion, as the Secretary of State shall determine.

(2) Paragraph (1) shall not apply where—
- (a) a person who is required to attend for, or submit to, a medical examination proves to the satisfaction of the Secretary of State that he has good cause for failing to comply with the requirement to attend for, or submit himself to, medical examination;
- (b) a person who is required to attend for, or submit to, a medical examination produces such evidence as is acceptable to the Secretary of State in place of a medical examination; or
- (c) the Secretary of State otherwise has available to him such evidence as is acceptable to him.

(3) For the purposes of paragraph (2)(a), the matters which are to be taken into account in determining whether a person has good cause shall include—
- (a) whether he was outside Great Britain at the relevant time;
- (b) his state of health at the relevant time; and
- (c) the nature of any disability from which he suffers.

## Payment of withheld benefit
**5C.—**

(1) Where the Secretary of State is satisfied that no question arises in connection with his investigation referred to in regulation 5A(1), payment of the amount withheld and the disability living allowance shall be made forthwith.

(2) Where a question arose in connection with an investigation referred to in regulation 5A(1) in respect of which—
- (a) the Secretary of State made an application for the review of a person's entitlement to disability living allowance under section 30 of the Administration Act; and
- (b) an adjudication officer has made a determination;

payment of the disability living allowance shall be made in accordance with the adjudication officer's determination, on review, of the person's entitlement.

(3) Where paragraph (1) or (2) does not apply and disability living allowance is withheld under regulation 5B for a period of more than 3 months, the Secretary of State shall—
- (a) make, with a view to review, an application to the adjudication officer on the ground that the person failed to attend for, or submit himself to, medical examination; and
- (b) make such payments as are determined, on review, by the adjudication officer."

**p. 655,** *annotations to regulation 8*

This regulation disqualifies a claimant who is being treated in a publicly financed hospital. In Decision *CDLA/11099/1996* the Commissioner had to decide if it applied to a patient who spent each night in such a hospital but was at home through the day. He held that it did; because the claimant spent a part of each day in a publicly funded hospital he could not qualify for benefit on any day.

**p. 668,** *add to the list of amending and revoking regulations:*

Social Security (Attendance Allowance and Disability Living Allowance) (Miscellaneous Amendments) Regulations 1997 (S.I. 1997 No. 1839).

**pp. 920–922,** *regulations 6–8: the importance of the MED4*

Although from the terms of these regulations, the provision of a MED 4 appears essential to support a claim, failure to supply one does not prevent the AO from subjecting the claimant to an all work test medical examination and making a decision in the light of that, and any other evidence, on whether the claimant does or does not satisfy the all work test (*CIB15235/96*, starred as *51/ 97*) especially paragraphs 10–16.

**pp. 934–935,** *annotation to regulation 21: the inquisitorial role of the SSAT*

In *CIB/14442/96* (starred as *43/97*), Commissioner Howell, setting aside the SSAT decision as erroneous in law for inadequate reasoning in the face of the medial evidence before it, considered the role of the SSAT in incapacity benefit cases:

> "I would emphasise that in incapacity benefit cases just as much as in other appeals coming before tribunals under the Social Security Acts, the function of the tribunal is an inquisitorial one, whose object is the ascertainment of the claimant's true entitlement and the determination of all relevant questions whether or not these have been formally put in issue before them. In the present case there was at least some cause for further question about whether the descriptors picked by the adjudication officer truly reflected the extent of the claimant's disability in view of the state of the medical evidence by the time that matter came before the tribunal at the hearing. I do not think that in all cases the tribunal should regard the scope of their enquiries as circumscribed by the boxes claimants may or may not have ticked at an earlier stage on the long and very complicated forms they are now required to fill out. That the form apparently did cause this claimant some confusion is evidenced from the fact that she ticked two descriptor boxes against "bending and kneeling" on page 11, one of which would have given her 15 points in its own right and the other only three. In my judgment, the tribunal should have gone further into this question (on which the condition of the claimant's knee, shoulder and lower back was of course of crucial importance) rather than simply recording the lower scoring descriptor as "agreed" as they did on page 57.
>
> 16. By the same token, although on page 13 she had only ticked the box that indicated she had difficulty with her left arm, the comments she added about her difficulties with lifting should in my view have alerted the tribunal to the possibility that she might have equal difficulty with lifting potatoes or other things with *either* arm, in view of the pull this would impose on her shoulder...." (paragraphs 15, 16).

Note, however, Commissioner Goodman's warning in *CIB/14202/1996* (starred as *42/97*) to proceed cautiously in the sphere of mental disablement (see update to page 953, below). Note further, that SSATs should consider matters down to the date of the hearing: see *CIB/14430/96(T)* (starred as *66/97*) noted in the update to page 23, above.

**pp. 936–938,** *tasks for the SSAT*

Note that the SSAT here as elsewhere has an inquisitorial role (*CIB/14442/96*, starred as *43/97*, update to pages 934–935, above), which it should be cautious in exercising when considering mental disablement (*CIB/14202/1996*, starred as *42/97*, update to page 953, below), and that it should consider matters down to the date of the hearing (*CIB/14430/96(T)*, starred as *66/97*, update to page 23, above).

**pp. 937–938,** *regulation 24: the all work test and the importance of the MED4*

Although from the terms of regulations 6–8 and 28, the provision of a MED 4 appears essential to support a claim, failure to supply one does not prevent the AO from subjecting the claimant to an all work test medical examination and making a decision in the light of that, and any other evidence, on whether the claimant does or does not satisfy the all work test (*CIB15235/96*, starred as *51/97*), especially paragraphs 10–16.

**pp. 943–944,** *regulation 28: the importance of the MED4*

Although from the terms of this regulation (and regulations 6–8), the provision of a MED4 appears essential to support a claim, failure to supply one does not prevent the AO from subjecting the claimant to an all work test medical examination and making a decision in the light of that, and any other evidence, on whether the claimant does or does not satisfy the all work test (*CIB15235/96*, starred as *51/97*) especially paragraphs 10–16.

**pp. 951–952,** *annotations to the Schedule: the proper approach to the statutory wording, the effect of pain, the concept of reasonable regularity and the relevance of the "working situation"*

A number of propositions on these matters seem to be emerging from the case law, but as yet it is not possible to say that they command the general agreement of Commissioners, being set out in starred decisions, awaiting a decision on whether they will be reported. A broad rather than literal approach to interpretation should be adopted. Assessment must take into account the effects of pain. A concept of "reasonable regularity" applies in respect of ability to perform tasks in the descriptors, something which perhaps reflects that this is a test of capacity for work. But there is no extra test of ability to carry them out in a specific work environment. Note, however, on this last matter of the relevance of a "work environment", Commissioner Goodman, while declining to comment in detail on those cases rejecting testing in the "work environment", has stated that he "would wish to consider the matter carefully if it became critical, bearing in mind that the whole of the Schedule to the 1995 Regulations is headed 'Disabilities which may make a person incapable of work' ". (*CIB/14332/1996* (starred as *38/97*, paragraph 12), a comment which may indicate that the final boundaries concerning the role, if any, of the "work situation" have yet to be drawn. Subject to that, it is appropriate to consider the relevant cases in some detail, so far as possible in the words of the individual Commissioners themselves, since their formulations, even where generally agreeing on the propositions summarised above, contain subtle differences of emphasis.

Chief Commissioner Chambers in the Northern Ireland decision *CI/95(1B)* (noted in (1996) 3 J.S.S.L. D176–177) ruled that the fact that the all work test is one of incapacity for work, means that in approaching whether someone can perform a particular task implies that the person must be able to do so "with reasonable regularity". He also held that otherwise an SSAT should not have regard to a "working situation", but should confine their consideration to the claimant's ability to perform the everyday activities specified in the descriptors (*ibid.*)

Both propositions were endorsed by Commissioner Walker in *CSIB/17/96* (starred as *26/97*): in paragraph 10 of that decision he stated

> "On the question of the use of a pen, I regard the tribunal's approach as faulty. That an individual managed to complete a form does not necessarily and simply mean, as the tribunal seemed to have concluded, that a pen or pencil could be used. Applying the Northern Ireland Chief Commissioner's approach, that has to be determined in the light of reasonableness and some regularity. The evidence before the tribunal was that the claimant did complete the form using a pen—"but it took a while". That qualification should have been explored. It may be that even so the claimant was in a general way able to use a pen or a pencil. But if the "while" was sufficiently long or if there were breaks or rests it may be that the answer should be otherwise. The tribunal decision is further defective in law because they have not dealt as fully as they should with these matters."

The further matter arose of the claimant's ability to use a kettle. It was common ground between the parties that his specially adapted kettle was not the one to focus on; the focus should (at the very least) be on a normal one. The claimant's representative, however, argued that

> "the proper context within which to determine the descriptors was that of a working situation. Thus, he submitted that kettle pouring or saucepan pouring should be considered in the context of a commercial kitchen. . . . [A]lthough this is described as the "all work test", I have no doubt that the Chief Commissioner in Northern Ireland was correct when he determined in the case cited that an appeal tribunal should not have regard to such a factor but should confine their considerations to ability to perform the everyday activities specified in the descriptor. That, as it seems to me, is so because the range of descriptors taken as a whole [is] designed to give an overall picture of an individual' general ability or inability to undertake activities which may bear upon a general working situation. It seems to me that the purpose of the scheme is sufficiently obvious, namely that if sufficient descriptors are satisfied there is probably little useful work or employment which an individual could either do or obtain. I therefore direct the new tribunal to apply the descriptors generally in line with the foregoing guidance, but not in a working situation" (paragraph 13).

Further support is found in Commissioner Rice's decision in *CIB/14587/1996* (starred as *65/97*) in which "bending and kneeling" was at issue. The claimant had told the SSAT that he could bend and kneel "but not repeatedly". It was unclear from the tribunal's decision why they had rejected that and accordingly the Commissioner set the decision aside as erroneous in law. He than proceeded to give guidance on how a differently constituted SSAT should approach the appeal:

> "There would seem to be no doubt that the claimant is capable of bending and kneeling. However, can he do so without discomfort, and can he do so with reasonable frequency? For I do not think it is enough to treat him as capable of bending and kneeling if he can only do so subject to excruciating agony or, if having bent or knelt once, he is unable to repeat the exercise for hours or days thereafter. It is all a matter of degree. Can he bend or kneel without, at least too much discomfort, and can he repeat the exercise within a reasonable time. In other words, can he in the general sense of the word, in the course of his normal everyday activities, be said to be capable of bending and kneeling? It will be a matter for the tribunal to determine." (paragraph 7)

Commissioner Rice thus endorses the reasonable regularity approach supported in the annotation and in the above-mentioned cases. He also in effect supports the submission in the annotation that functions that can only be performed with more than an acceptable pain or discomfort are not to be regarded as within a claimant's capacity. But the claimant's representative had sought to persuade the Commissioner to go further, arguing that ability to bend and kneel should be judged in a "work context" or a "work environment". His argument drew support from this being a test of capacity for work and from the following statement in paragraph 17 of the "Medical Services Incapacity Benefit Handbook for Medical Services Doctors:"

> "There will be instances where the claimant can carry out an activity, but the activity promotes moderate pain. Consider whether the client could carry out such an action reliably, safely and repeatedly in the workplace. Reasonable risk cannot be ignored, and if, for example, the client would be at risk of falls when climbing stairs, this should be taken into account."

Commissioner Rice rejected the argument made by the claimant's representative. Drawing support from Chief Commissioner Chambers in *C1/95(IB)*, the Commissioner instead ruled that

> "The 'All Work Test' consists of a variety of tests as to a claimant's physical capacity under various heads. Shortcomings will result in the award of points, and if the claimant obtains 15 points or more, he will have satisfied the 'All Work Test' and will be deemed to have demonstrated his incapacity for all forms of work. *But these individual tests relate to the claimant's capacity to carry out ordinary functions in everyday life.* They are a convenient means of assessing the claimant's physical condition, on the basis of which he can, depending on the results, be treated as either capable or incapable of work. The individual tests are not themselves to be evaluated on the basis that, at the time they are applied, the claimant

is deemed to be at work, and subject to the normal demands of his employment. Thus, his ability to bend or kneel will not be subject to the requirements and pressure incidental to employment; *it will be adjudged by reference to the nominal needs of everyday living at home.*

12. It should also be mentioned that if a claimant's capacity to carry out the activities appearing in the Schedule were to be evaluated in a 'work context', difficulty would arise in determining which was the particular work context applicable to the claimant in question. What form of employment was he expected to undertake, on the basis of which the tests were to be judged? In my view this kind of difficulty has been deliberately sidestepped by *requiring the tests to be evaluated from the standpoint of general every-day living"* (paragraphs 9, 12, emphasis added by commentator).

Commissioner Howell also considered the matter in decisions *CIB/13161/96* and *CIB/13508/96* (starred together as *29/97*). These are crucial decisions in respect of the proper approach to cases concerning claimants who are intermittently incapable of work, who would clearly satisfy the all work test on some days, but equally clearly fail it on others, a matter discussed below (update to page 952).

Commissioner Howell supports the "everyday activities" approach, rejecting the working environment aspect insofar as creating a separate and additional test over and above the statutory wording, but not, it is submitted, insofar as a reference to the work context might import a particular common sense approach to the interpretation of words used therein (*e.g.* "can/cannot"):

"While the heading to the schedule and its legislative context identify its sole reason for existing as being to test for disablement from work, the fourteen activities themselves are specified in entirely general terms. They consist of things like walking, sitting, standing, bending, lifting, reaching and so forth that are in no way restricted to a work situation. The descriptors too refer only to commonplace situations in daily life such as turning a knob on a cooker, using a pen or carrying a carton of milk or a bag of potatoes, and are obviously intended to reflect a measurement of only the most basic physical and manual skills. *There is no indication or apparent scope for any separate or more substantive inquiry into how far a claimant's condition has really depleted his working skills, or whether those he has left are saleable in any real sense to an employer....*

40. As the Chief Commissioner [for Northern Ireland] points out there is no warrant in the regulations for a separate consideration of whether the claimant could or could not perform the listed activities in some imaginary working context such as a factory, if this means that some additional test is to be imported over and above that of whether the claimant can normally perform these activities in the sense that I have indicated. *I am not sure however that the tribunal in that case was really doing more than using their reference to a working context as a common sense reason to justify importing the concept of reasonable regularity approved in the passage [from C1/95(IB)] quoted above. A mere reference to work in that sense would not amount to using it as a separate factor.*

42. *Nor in my judgment is there any ground for attempting any kind of quantitative assessment of the number of different working situations a claimant might be able to cope with. That would be going beyond the plain intention to focus only on the ability to perform the list of everyday tasks,*

as the yardstick for a common sense assumption that if a person is not seriously handicapped in these, there must be at least some kind of work he could do. *Consideration of the requirements for specific jobs, and the kind of evidence that occupied so much time before tribunals under the old law, (with adjudication officers coming up with specimen job descriptions of very simple jobs that could be performed by anyone, and claimants coming up with detailed reasons why they thought them unsuitable) are now irrelevant*" (paragraphs 3, 40, 42, emphasis and square bracket references added by commentator)

As regards matters of repetition and the effect of pain, Commissioner Howell's starting point is a concept of normality and he adopts the approach of the Chief Commissioner for Northern Ireland on reasonable regularity:

"In my judgment, the context in which this new benefit test was introduced, and the use of a very basic set of mundane everyday activities intended to test whether a person can really be said to be incapable of any work at all, mean that by necessary implication the simple language used must be read in a reasonably broad and not a restricted literal sense. I do not think it is reading anything into regulation 24 to say that the test is one of the extent to which the disease or disability from which the claimant suffers impairs his normal capacity to perform the stated activities as compared with a person of normal capabilities in full working order.

38. The word "normal" appears twice in that last sentence, and it is in my view the key to applying the various descriptors in accordance with the legislative intention. Thus in my judgment the score of 15 points for "Cannot walk up and down a flight of 12 stairs" is applicable to a person who cannot normally do this as and when called upon to do so. It is not necessary to find that he is so incapacitated that he simply could not manage ever to get up a dozen stairs, even with the most supreme effort on one isolated occasion to avoid some terrible danger. For that matter there is no definition of what is meant by "stairs" in the schedule: but no reasonable person could have any difficulty in reading by implication that these are assumed to be stairs of normal size, breadth and grip, not some imaginary set of steep awkward metal stairs in something like a ship's engine room. Similarly the descriptor "cannot use a pen or pencil" in activity 7 ("Manual dexterity") must mean by necessary common sense implication that the claimant scores the points if he is physically unable to use a pen or pencil to write in a normal manner. A fair reading does not need the schedule itself to spell out that this is what is meant, rather than a total inability to wield a pen or pencil for any purpose at all, even punching a hole in a sheet of paper.

39. The question of how far the descriptors are to be intended to measure a claimant's ability to perform the stated tasks on a repeated basis and without pain must in my judgment be answered in the same empirical way" (paragraphs 37–39).

The Commissioner then cited with approval the passage from *C1/95(IB)* quoted on page 952 of the main work, but was of the opinion that the reference in it

"to a claimant being able to accomplish a task "most of the time" is . . . to be read in its context as meaning that the claimant would normally be able to perform the stated activity if and when called upon to do so. Consistently with this, the possibility of pain and fatigue and the increasing difficulty of performing an activity on a repeated basis must in my judgment be taken into account by considering how far the claimant's normal capabilities are impaired by comparison with those of a healthy person in normal working order. Even a fit man will suffer fatigue and his knees will start to ache if you make him walk up and down stairs many times in succession. The choice of descriptor should take into account whatever effects pain and fatigue may have on the claimant's ability to perform the task so far as they are beyond the normal by reason of his specific disability. The words "most of the time" are not to be taken as giving rise to some need to try and calculate percentages of successful or failed attempts over any real or imagined period."

**p. 952,** *intermittent conditions and practical loss of earning capacity*

In April, this commentator suggested that "difficult questions of judgment will arise where a claimant can sometimes do things, but at other times not. Presumably all one can do is to look at the picture which is usual or which prevails for the preponderance of the period." Commissioner Howell's "normality approach" (see update to pages 951–952, above) deals with one aspect of the problem: the reference in *C1/95(IB)* "to a claimant being able to accomplish a task 'most of the time' is . . . to be read in its context as meaning that the claimant would normally be able to perform the stated activity if and when called upon to do so." The more difficult situation is where it is accepted that the claimant's condition is such that for certain periods he is able to cope satisfactorily with most normal activities. Commissioner Howell considered two such cases in the appeals *CIB/13161/96* and *CIB/13508/96* (starred together as *29/97*). His solution to the problem is a logical one in terms of the structure of incapacity benefit as a daily benefit paid for any day of incapacity for work within a period of incapacity for work [see further main volume, pages 118–120 (a brief overview of incapacity benefit) and pages 124–128 (C & BA 1992, s.30C and annotations)]. But it is one that is liable to create evidentiary difficulties for claimants and SSATs unless and until the information supplied to claimants makes it clear that they must keep a daily "log" or "diary" to support their claim.

In *CIB/13161/96* the claimant suffered from Menieres disease. This is a disease of the inner ear giving rise to intermittent attacks of vertigo, nausea and extreme dizziness such that while they occur the claimant would typically not be able to stand, walk or manage stairs reliably, and could not do any kind of work, let alone his former occupation of glazier and decorator. The medical examination for the "all work test" took place, he alleged, in an asymptomatic period and he argued that the SSAT which had returned a score of "nil points" ought to have looked beyond the results of that examination to take account of the intermittent nature of his condition and to make a realistic assessment of whether he was capable of going out to work. The claimant in *CIB/13508/96* had until 1992 been a plasterer. He suffered from multiple joint arthritis which, varying in its impact, at times made it extremely difficult for him to move his shoulders and arms. Coupled with restricted movement in his spine the condition made it difficult for him to work at all reliably. Plastering, of course, requires the energetic movement of the parts of the body concerned. The SSAT which considered his case held him to satisfy the "all work test" with a score of 23 points.

Commissioner Howell set aside as erroneous in law both SSAT decisions as providing insufficient and unclear reasoning for the decisions. Having considered the legislative framework, structure and nature of incapacity benefit, he then, in aiming to give guidance to the differently constituted SSATs to which the cases were remitted, had to consider a number of questions on the application of the "all work test" which governed these claimants at this point in their incapacity claims. Both were transferees from invalidity benefit who had satisfied the tests then applicable: no work or type of work which the claimant could reasonably be expected to do; as the Commissioner put it, "entitlement to [invalidity benefit] thus depended on whether the claimant's condition had in a practical sense robbed him of his earning capacity". For incapacity benefit purposes, however, the cases gave rise to a number of questions concerning the application of the "all work test":

> "These questions were how the word 'cannot' is to be read, whether the tests are to be assumed to be applied in a working environment, to what extent the issue of practical employability of the claimant plays a part in the test at all" (paragraph 36)

Commissioner Howell's approach to these three questions has been considered alongside other Commissioners' decisions in the update to pages 951–952, above. Here one needs to consider the last of the questions he identified

> "how one is supposed to deal under the new legislation with an intermittent condition which renders the claimant incapable of reasonable work in the practical sense recognised by the previous law, but likely to attain equally valid scores of either a large number of points on the descriptor scale, or a very few or even none, depending on the day you happen to take into account for the testing" (paragraph 36)

The question was of importance not just to the claimants in the case or those with the exact same conditions but also with a number of other "intermittent, fluctuating or unpredictable medical conditions that make normal employment impossible", for example, multiple sclerosis and epilepsy. The answer given by the Commissioner identifies a legislative omission, arguably not the will of Parliament, which deprived these two claimants of the insurance cover the invalidity benefit regime had formerly given them:

> "it is, I think, inescapable that the legislation as it stands requires the all work test to be satisfied on a day to day basis for each individual day of claim before it can count as a "day of incapacity" and give rise to an entitlement to benefit. By requiring the test to be satisfied on a day to day basis but assuming (wrongly) that a constant measure of physical disabilities can be got from the descriptor table, it thus largely ignores the problem of people who have "good days and bad days" " (paragraph 44)

Clearly unhappy with the result the "all work test" produced in these types of cases in the context of incapacity benefit as a daily benefit for any day of incapacity in a period of incapacity for work, the Commissioner stated:

"Omission or not, it is a matter of concern and surprise that cover should have been withdrawn from a whole class of people in this way, going well beyond what might fairly have been thought necessary to correct any individual laxity in the application of the previous conditions. I recommend therefore that the particular problems of people rendered practically unemployable by serious but intermittent conditions be reconsidered as a matter of urgency by the Secretary of State."

Until re-appraisal takes place and its results are translated into legislation, how are SSATs to approach and deal with this type of case? Commissioner Howell's answer is simple to state but likely to prove something of a nightmare to carry out since most people do not keep a day-by-day log or diary of the disabling effects of their condition and appeals may well focus on a considerable time-period, not just the dates identified in the AO's decision but the period down to the date of the SSAT hearing [see further update to page 23, above]. That a rough and ready assessment may be acceptable is of some assistance to SSATs, but the process, as the Commissioner recognises, will produce injustices and anomalies.

"Where the all work test applies, it must be satisfied on a day to day basis for each day of claim that is to count as a day of incapacity. In so applying it as regards any day, a broad and not literal reading of the actual descriptors is to be adopted, so as to test a person's normal level of ability to carry out the specified activities as and when called upon to do so, taking into account any additional limitations from pain, fatigue, etc. compared with a person not suffering the disability but otherwise similar [see further, update to page 951–952, above]. Where a person suffers from an intermittent condition such that the test produces different answers for different days, the legislation does not at present permit an overall view to be taken over a continuous period. All relevant days of incapacity need therefore to be identified, so far as practicable over the period down to the tribunal's own decision [see further update to page 23, above] so as to give the claimant and the adjudication officer as much guidance as possible on the proper entitlement under the new regulations.

48. *This last part of the exercise may well involve the tribunal in making some rough and ready assessments on the best evidence they have available*, and the answer will still be unsatisfactory for the claimants as they will dip in and out of entitlement according to the length and severity of the attacks of their condition and the number of days involved. The application of the minimum four day and maximum eight week requirements under [C & BA 1992] section 30C [the continuity and linking rules, see main volume pp. 124–128 will give rise to further anomalies. However a tribunal forced by the new regulations to ignore the fact of a continuous loss of earning power can at least ensure, in fairness to claimants deprived of a benefit they thought they had paid for, that those days when they are laid up in bed, unable to stand or otherwise on any view incapacitated by a sporadic condition are taken into account so far as properly can be done." (paragraphs 47, 48, emphasis and reference in square brackets added by commentator]

**p. 953,** *new annotation: the approach to Part II of the Schedule: mental disabilities*

As Commissioner Goodman stressed in *CIB/14202/1996* (starred as *42/97*), it must be remembered that the all work test is one of a person's incapacity by reason of some specific disease or bodily or mental disablement, to perform the activities specified in the Schedule:

> "In this context, therefore, the matters specified in Part II ... can qualify for 'points' only if they result from 'mental disablement' (regulation 24). In other words, they must not be mere matters of moods but must relate to a recognisable mental disablement, in the nature of an illness and not shared by healthy members of the population. The generality of such a phrase as 'often sits for hours doing nothing' (paragraph 15(b)], for example, must be restricted to such a state resulting from a definite mental disability" (*ibid.*, paragraph 8)

Accordingly, while SSATs have an inquisitorial function requiring them to investigate all relevant matters (see also *CIB/14442/96*, starred as *43/97*), they should be cautious in exercising it in the sphere of mental disablement. In the case before Commissioner Goodman, the tribunal had done so of its own accord and without being presented with any preceding evidence, medical or otherwise on the matter, relying merely on what the claimant said to them, although it was not clear whether the claimant's statements came in answer to questions put by the tribunal or not. Commissioner Goodman was of the opinion that SSATs

> "should be hesitant in going into the question of possible mental disabilities unless they have been raised beforehand and in addition there is some medical or similar evidence on the point....
> 6. When looking in isolation at the list of 'mental disabilities' in the Schedule ... it would be easy, without I hope being cynical, to say of almost anyone that they could acquire some points under the various descriptors. For example the descriptor 'Avoids carrying out routine activities because he is convinced they will prove too tiring or stressful,' could ... describe anyone at a given point of time. The same is true of the descriptor, 'Is scared or anxious that work would bring back or worsen his illness'. In view of the general nature of these descriptors, I consider that tribunals ought to be sure that they do have some corroborative evidence preferably medical evidence, on these points. They should be careful not to elevate to 'mental disabilities', for example a mere disinclination to do certain tasks or to go to work on a certain day or a disinclination for the society of one's fellow human beings on certain occasions" (paragraphs 5, 6)

Hence the Commissioner's stress, noted above, that application of a "mental disability" descriptor must be restricted to a state resulting from a definite mental disability, a matter now put beyond any doubt by regulation 25(3)(b) as amended from January 6, 1997, which states categorically "in determining the extent of a person's incapacity to perform any activity listed in ... Part II, it shall be a condition that the person's incapacity arises ... in respect of a disability listed in Part II, from some specific mental illness or disablement".

**pp. 953–954,** *case law on specific activities/descriptors*

*Activity 14 descriptors: "altered consciousness"*. The wording of this activity was narrowed to its current formulation with effect from January 6, 1997. Prior to that it read: "remaining conscious other than for normal periods of sleep". Throughout, however, each of its associated descriptors 14(a)–(f) has used the words "an involuntary episode of lost or altered consciousness".

In *CSIB/14/96* (starred decision *73/97*), Commissioner Walker considered the meaning of and the proper approach to "altered consciousness" in a case involving the pre-January 1997 wording of activity 14. The case turned on descriptors (a) and (b) (worded then as now), satisfaction of either of which would have given the claimant the necessary 15 points to satisfy the all work test. The relevant disabling condition was argued to be a series of severe and frequent headaches which necessitated the claimant lying down for periods of between half an hour and two hours, during which periods the claimant was unable to conduct his normal activities but did not lose consciousness. The question was whether, during these periods, the claimant could be said to have suffered "altered consciousness":

> "The crux of [the claimant's representative's] argument centred upon the degree of awareness of perception which an individual would normally have when conscious. If, he submitted, that awareness or perception became distorted or restricted by a degree of pain sufficient to that end then for the duration of that distorted or restricted awareness of perception the individual's consciousness could properly be said to have become 'altered'. He pointed to what was said for the guidance of the examining medical practitioner in the medical report form IB85, . . . a sheet headed 'Remaining conscious other than for normal periods of sleep'. There then followed the various descriptors. But between the activity and the descriptors this guidance is contained
> 'These include seizures, blackouts, faints and any disturbance of consciousness occurring while awake that prevents continuing activity'.
> [The claimant's representative's] point, at its simplest, was that if an individual suffered a degree of pain which disturbed his consciousness in the way submitted and prevented continuing activity then that amounted to the required 'involuntary episode'." (paragraph 6, words in square brackets supplied by commentator)

Commissioner Walker rejected the argument put on behalf of the AO that the phrase "lost or altered consciousness" should be read *ejusdem generis*, so that, while "altered" indicated something wider than "lost" nonetheless it took its colour from "lost". The Commissioner was not persuaded that the *ejusdem generis* rule applied and was satisfied "that the two concepts are different and fall to be constructed in the normal way as being two alternative conditions set out in a statutory provision", the "or" being merely disjunctive (paragraph 7). He set aside as erroneous in law the SSAT decision (which had gone against the claimant): their reasoning was insufficiently clear for the claimant or the Commissioner to see exactly whey they had made the decision they did. As to the meaning of "altered consciousness", he continued:

> "The discussion satisfied me that it is not possible to lay down guidelines as to what, in law, is meant by 'altered consciousness'. It is, I am equally

satisfied, essentially a practical matter for a tribunal to determine in the light of medical guidance from their assessor and the application of commonsense. But where, as here, episodes of pain are the disabling condition it will be necessary for the tribunal to explore, and for the claimant to present appropriate evidence to allow such exploration, in some detail how the pain affects the individual during an episode. It is not, in my view, sufficient to find as a fact that during the period 'the appellant is disabled'. Nor that 'he is unable to conduct his normal daily activities'. *It is for determination first how pain forecloses these and the way in which and the extent to which it does so. Thus ... if an individual is so distracted by the pain that he requires to lie down and otherwise retire from what he is doing then it may be possible to conclude that his consciousness has become altered by the degree of pain and he is incapable of doing anything effective other than coping with it.* But that would be a secondary finding which would require proper primary findings to justify it. Above all, I am persuaded that the concept of "altered consciousness", which may have some medical significance, is impossible of legal definition and is a concept of difficulty for application by lay tribunals. For these reasons I do not think that it is appropriate that I should give any further guidance to the new tribunal in this case." (paragraph 9, emphasis supplied by commentator)

The matter of giving substance to the concept "altered consciousness" and applying it to the facts of disputed cases is thus made very directly the task of the SSAT aided by its medical assessor and remain as relevant now as under the pre-January 1997 formulation, since the wording of the descriptors themselves remains unaltered. The Commissioner's highlighted comments about the effects and implications of severe pain in this context open up possibilities under activity 14 for, for example, those suffering frequent disabling migraines or very severe, back pain. The change to the current formulation of activity 14 removes that for any period from January 6, 1997. But those highlighted comments will be highly relevant in cases involving any period prior to that date, based on the then wider wording of the activity, but will require a careful approach to the evidence, to fact-finding, and to the appropriate conclusions to draw from the primary facts.

*Activity 13: Continence: "loses control of bowels":* applying the descriptors in the "all work test" involves intrusive scrutiny of the lives of claimants. Those in respect of activity 13 particularly so, embracing intimate and embarrassing areas affecting a claimant's dignity. Apparently some 20 per cent of the population suffer from irritable bowel syndrome (IBS), a condition which may have a disruptive and distressing effect on their personal lives and their ability to undertake work. A medical report from a consultant physician with considerable expertise cited in *CIB/14332/96* (starred as *38/97*) is very telling:

" ... Urgency of defecation is a well recognised symptom of Irritable Bowel Syndrome, but not one suffered by all patients with IBS. It is sometimes so severe that patients are restricted in their activities and afraid to go out. This urgency is disabling and perhaps 10–15 per cent of patients with IBS and a similar proportion are unable to work. You are of course right in saying that there is a wide range of severity and in the type of symptoms suffered by patients with IBS, ranging from mild discomfort to excruciating pain and mild bowel irregularity to severe irregularity suffered by [the claimant]. The urgency suffered by patients with IBS does occasionally lead to incontinence of faeces. You ask if there is a medical definition of losing control of the bowels. The term used by doctors is faecal incontinence and this covers everything from minor stain on the underpants when evacuating wind to liquid running down the legs. Obviously the distress caused by incontinence varies with its severity. However fear of incontinence is very severe in some people and has even made IBS patients suicidal. You ask if there is a medical definition of the bowel and does this include the external anal sphincter. The term bowel is not a precisely definable one and it is better to talk about the specific part of the intestines such as the small intestine, large intestine, rectum and anus. Obviously "bowel function" in the ordinary sense of the word is greatly determined by the efficiency and function of the anal sphincters (internal as well as external). Finally you ask if treatment of IBS with antidiarrhoeal drugs can lead to an increase in abdominal pain. The answer is yes it certainly can and this causes considerable problems in management."

In *CIB/14332/96* (starred as *38/97*), a decision which will give aid and comfort to severe IBS sufferers like the claimant in that case, Commissioner Goodman held that the term 'loses control of bowels' does not require a claimant to suffer a wet discharge, but "can comprehend a situation where a claimant does not in fact 'mess himself', provided he is able immediately to rush to a nearby lavatory" (paragraph 16), and the decision is a precedent for that proposition (*ibid.*). In thus supporting the decision of the majority of the SSAT in favour of the claimant, Commissioner Goodman drew on the distinction in the activity 13 descriptors (a) and (d) between 'no voluntary control of the bowels' and 'loses control of bowels' ". He also used as an aid to interpretation of the term a statement in paragraph 7 of the Benefit Agency's "Medical Services Incapacity Benefit Handbook for Medical Services Doctors":

"Clients with gastro-intestinal problems or frequency of micturition should be considered as having no voluntary control when their problem is such that they would become incontinent if they did not leave their work place immediately or within a very short space of time".

The Commissioner did not consider that decisions on disregarding the working situation (see update to page 952) precluded drawing on the statement as an interpretative aid (paragraph 13) and indeed gave some indication that he did not necessarily endorse the approach taken in those cases (paragraph 12). He considered that

"the expression loses 'control of bowels' is apt (as indeed the Handbook indicates) to include a situation like this where the claimant suffers from severe Irritable Bowel Syndrome. He loses control of his bowels at least once a month (indeed it appears once a week probably) in the sense that he is not able to 'hold himself', as the normal person can do even when faced with a considerable urge to defaecate. If the claimant did not immediately rush to the lavatory, he would indeed 'mess himself' " (paragraph 14)

The decision turns to a great extent on the facts of that particular case "and is not to be regarded as a precedent for a view that every sufferer from Irritable

Bowel Syndrome (which is widespread) could be said to fulfill any of the descriptors specified in paragraph 13). The likelihood is that the majority of such sufferers could not comply with any of those descriptors'' (paragraph 16). The case seems to be the first such brought before the Commissioners (paragraph 15). Other diseases like Crohn's Disease give rise to similar problems but ''must await decision when cases involving them arise'' (paragraph 16).

*Activity 7: manual dexterity: descriptor (d) "cannot use a pen or pencil":* In *CIB/16237/1996* (starred as *50/97*), Commissioner Rice noted that the rubric, unlike those in paragraphs (a)–(c) of activity 7 descriptors, does not include the words ''with either hand''. Despite that he did not consider that this meant

> ''that a person is entitled under descriptor 7(d) to 15 points if he cannot use a *pencil in each hand*. As most people can only use a pen or pencil in one hand, such a construction would make nonsense of the descriptor. Accordingly, I am satisfied that the test is whether or not a person cannot use a pen or pencil *with either hand*.
> 
> 7. Accordingly, if a person cannot use a pen or pencil for the purposes for which a pen or pencil is normally used with either the right or the left hand, depending on which is dominant, he will prima facie be entitled to 15 points. Of course, it may be that in unusual circumstances a person who is, for example right-handed and has lost the use of that hand for writing, has acquired a compensating skill in his left hand. If that is the case, then he will not satisfy the descriptor. It may be that his skill in the left hand is not as good as it was originally in the right hand, but provided he still attains a reasonable standard so that he could be said in everyday language to be able to use a pen or pencil to write reasonably clearly and at reasonable speed, as well as to accomplish other things such as ticking forms and signing his name, he will not be entitled to the 15 points. Seemingly in the case of an ambidextrous person, he will not satisfy the test, so long as he has sufficient use of *one* hand'' (paragraphs 6, 7, emphasis in the original).

In the case before the Commissioner, the claimant succeeded; he was right-handed, unable to hold a pen or pencil in that hand, and unable to use the same in his left hand to produce anything more than a scrawl, nothing legible (paragraph 8).

In *CIB/13161/96* and *CIB/13508/96* (starred together as *29/97*), Commissioner Howell commented

> ''the descriptor 'cannot use a pen or pencil' ... must mean by necessary common sense implication that the claimant scores the points if he is physically unable to use a pen or pencil to write in a normal manner. A fair reading does not need the schedule itself to spell out that this is what is meant, rather than a total inability to wield a pen or pencil for any purpose at all, even punching a hole in a sheet of paper'' (paragraph 38)

*Activity 2: walking up and down stairs:* In *CIB/13161/96* and *CIB/13508/96* (starred together as *29/97*), Commissioner Howell commented

> ''there is no definition of what is meant by stairs in the schedule, but no reasonable person could have any difficulty in reading by implication that these are assumed to be stairs of normal size, breadth and grip, not some

imaginary set of steep awkward metal stairs in something like a ship's engine room" (paragraph 38).

**p. 1030,** *annotations to regulation 2*

In *CF/7146/1995* the claimant had sent his three children abroad to Pakistan where they were to attend school for the next three years. By the time the appeal came to the Commissioner that school had been recognised by the Secretary of State as an educational establishment for the purposes of the regulation. However, at the hearing before the SSAT the claimant had explained that he was sending his children to Pakistan not only for education, but so that they could experience and absorb the cultural atmosphere of Pakistan. The Commissioner felt bound to uphold the finding of the SSAT that the children's absence was not "by reason only" of receiving education and that the claim therefore failed.

**p. 1039,** *annotations to regulation 2*

An attempt to obtain two payments at the higher rate in respect of twins failed in *R(F)2/96*. The boys had been born within 30 seconds of each other, but the Commissioner upheld the decision of the SSAT that only one enhanced payment was payable in respect of the (slightly) elder of them. The question does not yet seem to have been asked in respect of Siamese twins or possibly twins born by Caesarean section and removed together!

**p. 1089,** *a new annotation to prescribed disease A10(w) (occupational deafness)*

Starred decision *CI/12201/96* establishes that, apart from the reference to mineral wool in sub-paragraph (ii), the whole of the prescription in A10(w) is confined to glass manufacture. In that case, the claimant was a clay worker in the pottery industry. He operated a "forming machine, used in the manufacture of ceramic (pottery) *hollow ware*, but not *glass* hollow ware" (paragraph 4). The Commissioner rejected the argument of the claimant's representative that "hollow ware" was not confined to glass, but included metal and ceramics. Taking account of the Industrial Injuries Advisory Council Report [Cm. 817 (1994)] (which had led to the introduction of A10(w)) in order to interpret ambiguous wording in the legislative prescription, Commissioner Goodman came to the conclusion that the

> "prescription is (apart from mineral wool) confined to glass manufacture. The words, '... forming machines used in the manufacture of glass containers *or* hollow ware' do in my view read in such a way that the adjective 'glass' applies not only to 'containers' but also to 'hollow ware'. That is the natural meaning of the sentence and it also coincides with the fact that the rest of sub-paragraphs (i) and (ii) and (iii) of paragraph (w) are all clearly confined to the manufacture of various kinds of glass (save 'mineral wool' in sub-paragraph (ii)). The report of the Advisory Council leads to the same conclusion and I am entitled to look at its contents in view of the ambiguity introduced in [sub-] paragraph (i) of paragraph (w) by the use of the word 'or' between 'glass containers' and 'hollow ware'. Overall, therefore, I am satisfied that the tribunal arrived at the correct decision and that the prescribed occupation in paragraph (w) of Paragraph A10 is not

intended to apply to any kind of hollow ware except that made of glass. I must therefore dismiss the claimant's appeal accordingly." (paragraph 13)

**pp. 1089–1090,** *annotations to prescribed disease A12 (carpal tunnel syndrome)*

As noted, in the original *CI/5408/1995* (starred decision *8/97*), in March 1996, Commissioner Rice followed *CI/160/94*, and decided the appeal against the claimant, holding that the buffing machine operated by her was not a hand-held vibrating tool within the meaning of the legislative prescription. But his decision was given in ignorance of two of Commissioner Goodman's decisions on ostensibly similar machines: *CI/696/49* (a concrete floor scrubber) and *CI/514/94* (a floor buffer). When he became aware of those decisions, Commissioner Rice set aside his decision and the appeal was reheard before Commissioner Henty. The product is a new decision *CI/5408/1995* (starred decision 11/97). Commissioner Henty's decision reviews all the pertinent authorities. The decision is in favour of the claimant and follows the *ratio* of Commissioner Goodman's decisions. Its effect is that the approach to "hand-held" in the quotation from *CI/160/94* is seen as correct insofar as it prevents static, fixed machines of the type at issue in that case (on which hands merely rested) being within the prescription. The requirement of "portability" in that approach was seen as *obiter* (not necessary for that decision). Having reviewed the relevant cases and the relevant report of the Industrial Injuries Advisory Council on the prescription of carpal tunnel syndrome (March 1992), Commissioner Henty gave his reasoned opinion on what he found a very difficult question:

"All the previous decisions I have referred to are in agreement that a fixed machine, which requires the application of the hand to operate it, is not 'a hand-held tool'. However, it does not seem to me that there is much difference in fact between (i) a tool which vibrates and requires, during its operation, to be carried by hand either continuously or intermittently; and (ii) a tool which vibrates and, in its operation, requires to be moved either continuously or intermittently and that motion is provided by the energy of the operator. I exclude self-propelled machines. As I have pointed out, a buffing machine is self-supporting and is not mounted on some support. It is therefore clearly different from the fixed tools in *CI/160/94* and *CI/156/94* [both of which concerned fixed sewing machines]. For instance, a portable electric drill vibrates and, when in use, it has to be moved and firmly grasped by hand, and the operator, when drilling, is required to exert considerable pressure. In the same way, an industrial buffing machine vibrates, and, when in use, it has to be moved by the operator backwards and forwards, manoeuvred and guided, requiring a firm grasp, and the firmer the grasp, the more keenly will any vibration be transmitted. I have, therefore, come to the conclusion that an industrial buffing machine is within the definition of a hand-held vibrating tool . . .". (paragraph 14)

He was assisted in so concluding by the fact that when the opportunity was taken to effect a legislative modification to the prescription to vitiate the effect of *CI/227/94* and *CI/514/95*, no step was taken to remedy any dissatisfaction with Commissioner Goodman's decisions on hand-held, this indicating acceptance of the effect of those decisions (*ibid.*).

**p. 1109,** *regulation 3: circumstances in which a person over pensionable age is to be regarded as having given up regular employment*

This regulation came into force on March 24, 1996, the date on which it was inserted by the Social Security (Industrial Injuries and Diseases)(Miscellaneous Amendment) Regulations 1996. In decisions *CI094/94* and *CI600/94* (starred together as *46/97*), Commissioner Howell held that it removed entitlement to REA and replaced it with retirement allowance for life with effect from March 31, 1996 (the beginning of the week after March 24, 1996) even in the case of two ladies who had attained pensionable age prior to March 24 and had in normal parlance given up (but not retired from) regular employment because of incapacity long before either April 10, 1989 (the date in C & BA 1992, Schedule 7, paragraph 13(1)) or March 24, 1996 (the date regulation 3 came into force). The two ladies would not otherwise have been deprived of REA by paragraph 13(1) because of the fact that they had as at October 1, 1989 been long out of work so that they could not be said to have "given up" regular employment on any day on or after that date as paragraph 13(10(b) as supplemented by the original 1990 regulations required, "gives up" bearing its ordinary natural meaning (*R(I)2/93, R(I)3/93*). Regulation 3 did, however, deprive them of it and transfer them to retirement allowance by, albeit artificially, regarding them as having given it up. See in particular paragraphs 37, 38 and 40–49.

The case is very useful in charting the bumpy and twisting path of attempts to make entitlements to REA cease on retirement, and makes clear that regulation 3 is *intra vires* the rule making power in C & BA1992, paragraph 13(8). Note, however, that leave to appeal to the Court of Appeal was granted on September 8, 1997.

Since both ladies had attained the age of 65 before the regulation deprived them of REA, "the condition linked to pensionable age in paragraph 13(1) has no discriminatory effect", rendering it unnecessary in their case to consider any possible application of Council Directive 79/7 EEC (main volume, pages 374–378). Other case which do are pending before the Commissioners: see update to pages 267–268, above.